W9-AXL-544

CHARMING SMALL HOTEL GUIDES

SPAIN

CHARMING SMALL HOTEL GUIDES

SPAIN

Including Mallorca, Menorca, Ibiza, Formentera,
Lanzarote and Tenerife

EDITED BY

Nick Inman

Interlink Books
An imprint of Interlink Publishing Group, Inc.
New York • Northampton

7th expanded & redesigned edition

First American edition published in 2003 by
Interlink Books
An imprint of Interlink Publishing Group, Inc
46 Crosby Street, Northampton, Massachusetts 01060
www.interlinkbooks.com

Copyright © Duncan Petersen Publishing Ltd 2003, 2001, 2000,
1999, 1998

This series is conceived, designed and produced by
Duncan Petersen Publishing Ltd.,
31 Ceylon Road, London W14 OPY

Editorial Director Andrew Duncan
Editor Nick Inman
Associate Editor Clara Villanueva
Production Editor Nicola Davies
Art Editor Don Macpherson

Library of Congress Cataloging-in-Publication Data available
ISBN 1-56656-501-4

Printed and bound in Italy

CONTENTS

INTRODUCTION

Welcome to this new expanded edition of the *Charming Small Hotel Guide* to Spain. It's a decade since we first travelled every corner of the country to create the first edition of this guide. Then, to be honest, we were disappointed. It was hard to find two hundred of our kind of hotel – whereas in Britain, France and Italy, it was easy to write about well over three hundred.

In the intervening years, a small revolution has taken place in the Spanish hotel scene, in response to economic development and a renewed enthusiasm for the country by independent travellers of many nationalities. Dozens of charming old buildings from *fincas* (farmhouses) and olive presses to castles, monasteries and decaying patrician town houses have been revived to make what we would call genuine charming small hotels. And the standard has generally risen: many that were formerly sober and monumental have been softened and individualized.

This new edition of the guide reflects as many of these new developments as time has allowed. It also contains an unusual number of interesting comments on hotels by readers. As always, we've enjoyed these enormously; thank you for taking the trouble, and keep the comments flowing, especially as (see below) we are already at work on a further expanded next edition.

For the first time, we're featuring some great places in the Canary Islands. Other interesting newcomers can be found in or outside Seville (page 141, 142 and 150); there is a delightful new find in the much visited 'white town' of Ronda (page 175); and a great walking base at the edge of the Picos de Europa in northern Spain (page 36). All in all, we've found it easy to add some twenty new places for this edition; work is already in progress to add as many again for the next one.

Our criteria

Our selection criteria are the same in Spain as they are anywhere. We aim to include only those places that are in some way captivating, with a distinctive personality, and which offer a truly personal service. While being highly selective, we also give as broad a range of recommendations as possible, to suit all budgets; and as hotels are often fully booked, it is useful to have alternatives. For a detailed summary of our selection criteria, see opposite.

In Spain, as elswhere in Europe, we found many hotels which easily satisfied our highly selective approach, but there are a significant number which, though basically recommendable, for one reason or another fall short of our ideal. The description of each hotel makes this distinction clear. However, be assured that all the hotels in the guide are, one way or another, true to the concept of the charming small hotel. If you find any more, please let us know.

In making our selection, we have been careful to bear in mind the many different requirements of our readers. Some will be backpackers; others will be millionaires; the vast majority will fall between the two.

Charming and small

Ideally, our recommendations have fewer than 30 bedrooms, but this is not a rigid requirement. Many hotels with more than 30 bedrooms feel much smaller, and you will find such places in this guide. We attach more importance to size than other guides because we think that unless a hotel is small, it cannot give a genuinely personal welcome, or make you feel like an individual, rather than just a guest. Unlike other guides, we often rule out places that have great qualities, but are nevertheless no more nor less than – hotels. Our hotels are special in some way.

We think that we have a much clearer idea than other guides of what is special and what is not: and we think we apply these criteria more consistently than other guides because we are a small and personally managed company rather than a bureaucracy. We have a small team of like-minded inspectors, thoroughly rehearsed in recognizing what we want. While we very much appreciate readers' reports – see below – they are not our main source of information.

Whole-page entries

We rarely see all these qualities together in one place; but our warmest recommendations – whole-page, with photograph – usually lack only one or two of these qualities.

Half-page entries

Don't, however, ignore our half-page entries. They are very useful addresses, and all are charming small hotels. You can't have stars on every page.

SO WHAT EXACTLY DO WE LOOK FOR?

- *A peaceful, attractive setting in an interesting and picturesque position.*

- *A building that is either handsome or interesting or historic, or at least with a distinct character.*

- *Bedrooms that are well proportioned with as much character as the public rooms below.*

- *Ideally, we look for adequate space, but on a human scale: we don't go for places that rely on grandeur, or that have pretensions that could intimidate.*

- *Decorations must be harmonious and in good taste, and the furnishings and facilities comfortable and well maintained. We like to see interesting antique furniture that is there because it can be used, not simply revered.*

- *The proprietors and staff need to be dedicated and thoughtful, offering a personal welcome, without being intrusive. The guest needs to feel like an individual.*

No fear or favour
Unlike many guides, there is no payment for inclusion. The selection is made entirely independently.

How to find an entry
In this guide, the entries are arranged by province, and the provinces are clustered in convenient regional groups. The regions, and within them the provinces, are arranged in a sequence starting in the extreme north-west (La Coruña) and working west to east and north to south. The Canary Islands come last in the sequence.

To find a hotel in a particular area, simply browse through headings at the top of the pages until you find that area – or use the maps following this introduction to locate the appropriate pages. To locate a specific hotel or a hotel in a specific place, use the indexes at the back, which lists the entries alphabetically, first by name and then by place-name.

How to read an entry
At the top of each entry is a coloured bar highlighting the place, followed by a categorisation which gives some clue to its character. These categories are, as far as possible, self-explanatory. The

letters PT in the name of a hotel stand for Parador de Turismo de España.

Fact boxes
The fact box given for each hotel follows a standard pattern: the explanation that follows is for full- and half-page entries.

Tel and Fax The first part of the number given in our entries is the area code within Spain. When calling from the UK dial 00 34; from the US, 001 34, then the full number.

E-mail This is becoming more and more popular; a quick and efficient way to book for both parties.

Websites are listed when available.

Location The location and setting of the hotel are briefly described and any useful information included to help you find your way there. Where parking is provided or available, we have made a note.

Meals Under this heading we list the meals available on the premises.

We do not state whether a hotel provides room service, as this can vary. If in doubt, check in advance with the selected hotel.

Prices We use price bands rather than figures:

€	under 30 euros
€€	30-60 euros
€€€	60-80 euros
€€€€	over 80 euros

Normally we give the range of prices you can expect to pay for a room, including tax and service – from the cost of the cheapest single room in low season to the cost of the dearest double in high season. Wherever possible we have given prices for 2000, but prices may be higher than those quoted because of inflation. But bear in mind also that the proprietors of hotels and guest-houses may change their prices from one year to another by much more than the rate of inflation. Always check when booking.

After the room price, we normally give the prices of breakfast and other meals. If room-only or bed-and- breakfast terms are not

EXCHANGE RATES
As we went to press, £1 sterling bought 1.58 euros and $1 U.S. bought 1.02 euros.

available, we give either the price for dinner, bed and breakfast (DB&B), or for full board (FB) – that is, all meals included:

€   under 10 euros
€€   10-25 euros
€€€   under 25 euros

Unless half-board is obligatory in a hotel, we have not mentioned its cost. But it is always worth asking in advance, because there are some very good deals to be had, especially over two- and three-day stays.

Above all, check the price first. Sometimes prices go up after we have gone to press. Sometimes there is a seasonal or other variation from the printed version.

Rooms Under this heading we indicate the number and type of room – and whether the rooms have baths (usually with shower or shower attachment as well) or just showers.

Facilities Under facilities we list: public rooms, lift, courtyard; garden, terrace or sitting-out area; outdoor or indoor swimming pool; tennis court; sauna, steam room, and fitness facilities.

Credit cards We use the following abbreviations:
AE   American Express
DC   Diners Club
MC   MasterCard (Access)
V   Visa (Barclaycard/Bank Americard)

Children Children are often welcome, but not always, and where this is so we have made note. We have made a distinction between children being 'welcome' and children being 'accepted'. Many private houses with precious antiques and furnishings would rather not accept children; others have guests who have come for peace and quiet. Some hotels and households do not like children in the dining-room in the evenings, and provide high tea at 6pm.

Disabled Many of our entries welcome disabled guests although they do not have special facilities; many have special facilities. We have noted where there are ground floor bedrooms or a lift.

Closed There is quite a variety of closing times and the dates we have given are those supplied to us by the hotel or guest house.

The final entry in the fact box is the name of the **Proprietor(s)**. Where the hotel is run by a manager, we give his or her name.

PARADORES

The state-run chain of Paradores dominates the Spanish hotel scene just as many of the castles the hotels occupy dominate the surrounding landscape. They are not the best hotels in Spain, and few of them are notably good by absolute standards – though in any given locality the Parador is quite likely to be the best in town, for the simple reason that many have been created in areas which private enterprise might not find attractive. But Paradores do have great attractions: many are set in wonderfully atmospheric old buildings – mansions, convents, hunting lodges as well as magnificent castles – and many others have spectacular mountain settings. Others are simply very convenient for the traveller on the road, being strategically positioned to fill gaps on the map of Spain.

In terms of their qualities as places to stay, Paradores are much less impressive. Their strong point, usually, is the bedrooms, which are normally very spacious and well furnished. Public rooms may be comfortable and inviting, but may equally be dismally furnished and gloomy. Food, which aims to reflect regional traditions, may be highly satisfactory or extremely ordinary. Service is equally unpredictable, and seems to depend more on individual initiative than any management policy.

Parador room prices vary widely (unlike meal prices, which are almost uniform). In the tourist Mecca of Granada, for example, you pay over three times what you pay in remote mountain areas; in most established tourist haunts – Toledo, Córdoba or Santillana del Mar, say – you pay something between these extremes.

Are they worth these prices? For most people, we judge that the answer is a qualified yes. The best of the Paradores – which you will be able to identify from our descriptions and photographs – really can add something to your travels. But we would not recommend planning a trip entirely around Paradores; not only would the cost mount up alarmingly, but the drawbacks of these somewhat inconsistent establishments might begin to weigh more heavily, while the special appeal that they have might begin to pall.

In our entries, we have abbreviated the proper name Parador de Turismo de España to the letters PT. Reservations for the Paradors can be made in the U.K.: Tel. 020 7616 0300. Fax 020 7616 0317.

REPORTING TO THE GUIDE

Please write and tell us about your experiences of small hotels, guest-houses and inns, whether good or bad, whether listed in this edition or not. As well as hotels in Spain, we are interested in hotels in Britain and Ireland, Italy, France, Portugal, Austria, Switzerland, Germany and other European countries, and those in the eastern United States.

The address to write to is:

> The Editor,
> c/o Duncan Petersen Publishing Ltd,
> 31 Ceylon Road,
> London W14 OPY.

Checklist
Please use a separate sheet of paper for each report; include your name, address and telephone number on each report.

Your reports will be received with particular pleasure if they are typed, and if they are organized under the following headings:

> Name of establishment
> Town or village it is in, or nearest
> Full address, including post code
> Telephone number
> Time and duration of visit
> The building and setting
> The public rooms
> The bedrooms and bathrooms
> Physical comfort (chairs, beds, heat, light, hot water)
>
> Standards of maintenance and housekeeping
> Atmosphere, welcome and service
> Food
> Value for money

We assume that in writing you have no objections to your views being published unpaid, either verbatim or in an edited version. Names of major outside contributors are acknowledged, at the editor's discretion, in the guide.

For visitors from outside Europe

First-time visitors to European countries, especially when they get to rural areas, are often surprised by the following:

- Facecloths and Kleenex tissues are not always provided as standard items.

- Private bathrooms with rooms aren't necessarily a standard feature.

- Floor numbers. What Americans call the first floor is known in Britain as the ground floor or 'O'.

- Elevators are known as lifts in Ireland.

- Parking lot is a term you won't encounter. You'll see 'Parking' or just a 'P' sign.

Figueras del Mar 31　Villavic
3
Neda 25　Ribadeo 26　Tox 27　Salas 28
Collia Arrio
La Coruña　　　　　Taramundi 34
Santiago 24　　　　○ Lugo　　　　　○
　　　　　　　　　　　　　　　Oviedo

● Villagarcia de Arosa 39
Cambados 38 ●　　　　　　　　　　　León
Villalonga 40 ●　● Pontevedra 41　　Astorga 46　　○
○ Vigo　○ Orense　Puebla de　Valencia de Don
　　　　　　Trives 43　　Juan 44 45
　　　Verin 42

○
Zamora

Salamanca ○

○ Ciudad Rodrigo

○ Cáceres

○ Badajoz

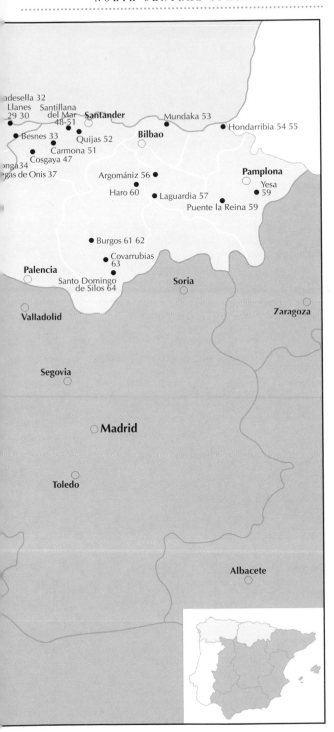

adesella 32
Llanes
29 30   Santillana
del Mar   **Santander**   Mundaka 53
48-51
Besnes 33   Quijas 52   **Bilbao**   Hondarribia 54 55
Carmona 51
Cosgaya 47

onga 34
gas de Onis 37   Argomániz 56   **Pamplona**
Haro 60   Laguardia 57   Yesa
59
Puente la Reina 59

Burgos 61 62

Covarrubias
63
Palencia
Santo Domingo   **Soria**
de Silos 64

Valladolid   **Zaragoza**

Segovia

Madrid

Toledo

Albacete

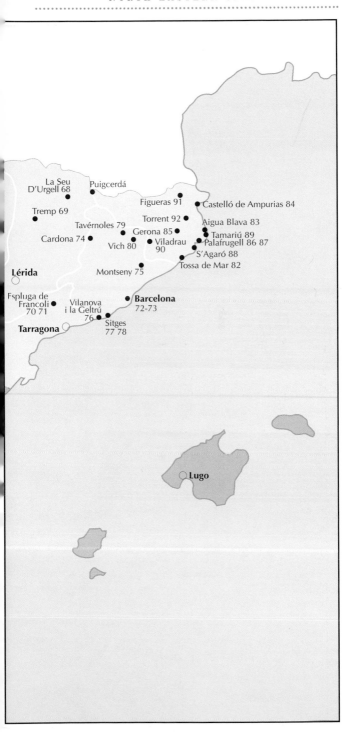

La Seu
D'Urgell 68   Puigcerdá

Tremp 69

Figueras 91   ● Castelló de Ampurias 84

Torrent 92 ●   Aigua Blava 83
Tavérnoles 79   Gerona 85 ●   ● Tamariú 89
Cardona 74 ●   Vich 80   ● Viladrau   Palafrugell 86 87
90   S'Agaró 88

Lérida   Tossa de Mar 82
Montseny 75

Espluga de
Francoli   Vilanova   ● **Barcelona**
70 71   i la Geltrú   72-73
76

Tarragona   Sitges
77 78

○**Lugo**

La Coruña

Oviedo

Santiago   Lugo

León

Vigo   Orense

Benavente 94 ●

Valladolid

Zamora 95 96

Salamanca ○

● Ciudad Rodrigo 97 98

Avila
111 112

● La Alberca 97

Jarandilla de la Vera 101 ●

Trujillo
102 103

Cáceres ○

Guadalupe 99-100

● Mérida 104 105

Badajoz

● Zafra 106

Córdoba

Seville

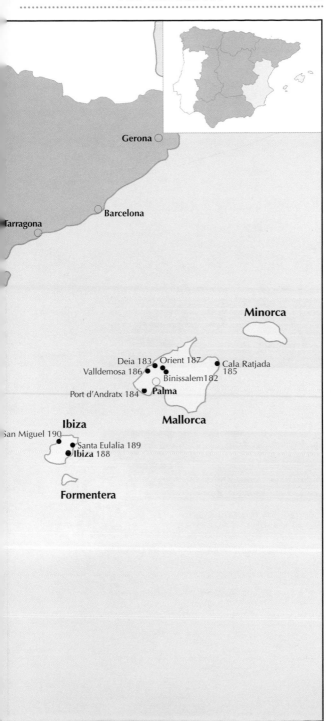

Gerona ○

Barcelona ○

Tarragona ○

Minorca

Deia 183 ● Orient 187 ● Cala Ratjada
Valldemosa 186 ● ● ● 185
Binissalem182 ○
Port d'Andratx 184 ● ● Palma

Mallorca

Ibiza
San Miguel 190 ● Santa Eulalia 189
● Ibiza 188

Formentera

Palencia

Valladolid

Zamora

Salamanca

Cuidad Rodrigo

Avila

Cáceres

Badajoz

Los Marines 137

Aracena 138

Córdoba 151

Seville 141-147

Palma del Rio 152

Aznalcazar 149

Carmona 139 140

Alcalá de Guadaira 148

Cruce de las Cabezas 150

Loja 160

Antequera 175

Sanlúcar de Barrameda 170-171

Chipiona

Jerez de la Frontera

Grazalema

Ronda 176

Málaga 1

Cádiz

Arcos de la Frontera 163-167

Benaojón 178

Ojén 179

Torremolir 174

Vejer de la Frontera 168

169

La Almoraima

Alhaurín el Grande 180

Tarifa 172

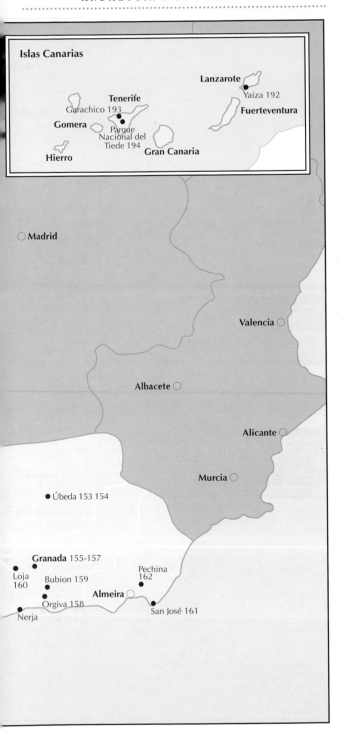

Islas Canarias

Lanzarote
Yaiza 192

Tenerife
Garachico 193

Fuerteventura

Gomera

Parque
Nacional del
Tiede 194

Gran Canaria

Hierro

○ Madrid

Valencia ○

Albacete ○

Alicante ○

Murcia ○

● Úbeda 153 154

Granada 155-157

Pechina
162

Loja
160

Bubion 159

Almeira ○

Orgiva 158

San José 161

Nerja

LA CORUÑA

La Estela

~ Bed and breakfast ~

Rajoy No 1, 15705, Santiago de Compostela, La Coruña
Tel (981) 582796

Santiago, with its relics of St James, has attracted pilgrims for centuries, and today people come for the beautifully preserved old city with its cathedral, squares and museums. This tiny, family-run hostal is tucked away in a corner right opposite one of Spain's most grand and opulent hotels (Los Reyes Católicos, now part of the Parador chain) – a rather interesting contrast, particularly if you compare prices. There is no restaurant here but the surrounding streets are packed with places to eat. The rooms are very basic but they are clean and quite adequate for a night's stop.

~

Nearby Cathedral, Old Town and the Hospital Real
Location in heart of old town, by Parador and cathedral; no private car parking
Prices rooms ⓔ; breakfast ⓔ
Rooms 5 double,4 with washbasin,1 with bath; 9 single, 3 with washbasin, 6 with bath; all rooms have central heating
Credit cards not accepted
Children welcome
Disabled no special facilities
Pets accepted **Closed** never
Proprietor Eduardo Pedrido

PARADORES IN NORTH-WEST SPAIN

NORTH-WEST SPAIN has more than its fair share of Paradores – and some of these are small and charming enough to have earned detailed entries. The province of Pontevedra (bordering Portugal on the west coast) is particularly well endowed, with four Paradores within a hundred kilometres of one another. The largest of these (122 rooms), the Parador de Bayona at Bayona, is a smart modern hotel built within the walls of an ancient fortress. It has all the classic ingredients – crenellated walls, pillared balconies, an open courtyard, richly decorated rooms, beautifully manicured lawns and spectacular views of the Ría de Vigo (Tel (986) 355000). By local standards Bayona is expensive, but it does not even come close to the Reyes Católicos in Santiago de Compostela – one of the most expensive Paradores, but also one of the most superior and most historic, built in the 15th century to house pilgrims from all over Europe who came to pay homage at the shrine of St James in Santiago's magnificent cathedral (Tel (981) 582200). Beware 25th July: this is the feast day of St James, and the city (and Parador) are packed.

Léon's central 253-room Parador, San Marcos, notable for its fabulous façade and two-storey cloisters and once a watering-hole on the pilgrim route to Santiago, is now a smart hotel, laden with antiques and surrounded by formal gardens (Tel (987) 237300).

La Coruña

Neda

Pazo da Merced

~ Country hotel ~

15510, Neda, La Coruña
Tel (981) 382200 **Fax** (981) 380104

Neda is a town full of beautiful old mansions, and this hotel, built of dressed stone, and with its own adjacent chapel, dedicated to the Virgen de la Merced (Our Lady of Mercy), is housed in one of them.

The pazo or country manor house, was built in the 17thC and sits in open countryside on the low-lying green shore at the head of the Ría del Ferrol.

A few years ago, the owners, facing bankruptcy, decided to sell it to an architect specializing in the restoration of old buildings. With patience and skill, he has turned it into a magnificent rural hotel which combines respect for the historic architecture with a certain originality in the use of materials. His wife, Marinela Medina, has taken charge of the management of the hotel.

The pazo only has five rooms, but they are well furnished and equipped with all that you could need. The service is welcoming and diligent: every guest is made to feel at home.

Through the windows you can see Couto monastery, with which the Pazo used to be connected by a tunnel underneath the water. The hotel makes a convenient base from which to visit this and other local examples of Romanesque architecture.

~

Nearby San Felipe castle (9 km); La Palma castle (14 km).
Location on the Ría del Ferrol, by the waterside; with garden and car parking
Meals breakfast
Prices rooms €€ - €€€; breakfast P
Rooms 5 double, all with bath; all rooms have central heating, TV,minibar, telephone, hairdrier
Facilities swimming-pool
Credit cards AE, DC, MC, V
Children very welcome **Disabled** access difficult **Pets** not accepted **Closed** never
Proprietor Marinela Medina

LUGO

RIBADEO

PT DE RIBADEO
～ MODERN PARADOR ～

Amador Fernández s/n, 27700, Ribadeo, Lugo
TEL (982) 128825 **FAX** (982) 128346

Ribadeo is now reached by an elegant road bridge which spans the mouth of the ria effectively bypassing the more picturesque towns of Figueras and Castropol which used to lie en route. The Parador finds itself in a quiet backwater of the town since the change in the traffic flow, but it is only a short walk into the town centre.

The building itself is nothing special and parts of it are showing their age. It overlooks the harbour which has the usual array of fishing boats, from one-man ventures to larger deep sea vessels, all bringing their catches right to the door. There is also a mineral-loading quay which can make clouds of dust if the wind is blowing the wrong way. The restaurant here, as you would expect, has an interesting selection of fish on the menu –also soups, salads, hors d'oeuvres, grills and stews.

The atmosphere here is informal, friendly and relaxed while offering all the more home-like Parador standards. One comment from a guest was surprise at the lack of spoken English on the reception desk, particularly as so many British use this hotel on their way to and from Galicia via Santander.

～

Nearby Early Romanesque Church of San Martín de Mondoñedo, near Foz (23 km); Los Castros beach (5 km).
Location above harbour in quiet part of town; with garden, garage and car parking
Meals breakfast, lunch, dinner
Prices rooms €€ - €€€€; breakfast €; dinner €€€
Rooms 42 double, 5 single, all with bath; all rooms have central heating, phone, TV, minibar
Facilities dining-room, sitting-room, 2 other sitting-areas, bar
Credit cards AE, DC, MC, V
Children welcome **Disabled** access easy; 2 ground-floor rooms
Pets not accepted **Closed** never
Manager Eligio Dominguez

ASTURIAS

Tox

VILLA BORINQUEN
~ COUNTRY HOTEL ~

Tox, , Villapedre, Asturias
TEL (98) 5648220 **FAX** (98) 5648222

This delightful hotel could not be more secluded – even the village of Tox does not appear on most maps (look for Villapedre). Between the main coast road and the shore, the Villa Borinquen sits quietly, unsignposted, amid rolling green cultivated land, far from any distractions.

It is a modern building, based on the houses of the wealthy Spaniards who returned from the Americas in the heyday of Spanish colonialism, and everything has been put together with comfort in mind. The bedrooms are enormous, and some have huge balconies overlooking the countryside and the extensive gardens to the sea. They are all carefully and individually furnished with large beds, comfortable armchairs, long drapes at the windows and rugs on the polished wood floors.

The hotel provides breakfast and snack meals, and the same management runs a restaurant down the road at the pretty little village of Puerto Vega, which has something of the atmosphere of a Cornish fishing village. Fish and shellfish are unloaded straight into the kitchen; you can watch the harbour at work as you eat and take a stroll along the sea wall as the sun goes down.

~

Nearby Barayo beach (5 km); the dramatic Navia valley (10 km).
Location in open fields near village, 1 km N of N634, about 11 km W of Luarca; with grounds and car parking
Meals breakfast
Prices rooms €€ - €€€€; breakfast P
Rooms 7 double, 1 single, 3 family rooms, all with bath; all rooms have central heating, phone, TV, minibar, hairdrier
Facilities sitting-room, breakfast-room, bar; mountain bikes
Credit cards MC, V
Children welcome; games available **Disabled** access easy; lift/elevator
Pets not accepted
Closed Jan
Manager Elisa Méndez

ASTURIAS

SALAS

CASTILLO DE VALDÉS-SALAS

～ HISTORIC TOWN HOTEL ～

Plaza de la Campa, s/n, 33860, Salas, Asturias
TEL (98) 5832222 **FAX** (98) 5832229

The market town of Salas is off the busy and tortuously winding road between Oviedo and the coast, in the foothills of the Cordillera Cantabrica. The town's 16thC castle has been restored and converted into a small and simple hotel, keeping much of the character of the original building intact

The massive doors lead you through the thick walls into the reception area, which also houses the local tourist information desk (both offering good spoken English). The building is constructed around a paved court-yard, with covered cloisters to shelter you from the mountain rain and from the summer sun. On the ground floor, off this patio area, is the cafe-teria/restaurant, whch is open to the public and serves unfussy dishes with local touches – try their cakes made with rice, milk and sugar, served with freshly brewed coffee. The bedrooms are mostly on the first floor and are very plain but stylish, with shutters at the windows, wooden floors and modern bathrooms tiled in red and white. There are two sitting-rooms upstairs; one has a television, games and books, and both have open fires in the winter. All the windows are double-glazed too, so it should be snug.

～

Nearby Benedictine monastery of San Salvador, Cornellana (10 km); viewpoint at Tineo (24 km).
Location in village just off N634, about 45 km W of Oviedo; with garden and car parking in square
Meals breakfast, lunch, dinner
Prices rooms €€; breakfast P; meals €€
Rooms 12 double, all with bath; all rooms have central heating, phone
Facilities dining-room, 2 sitting-rooms, bar, terrace
Credit cards AE, MC, V
Children accepted **Disabled** access difficult
Pets not accepted
Closed Jan
Proprietor Manuel López

ASTURIAS

LLANES

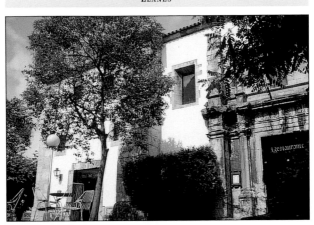

HOTEL DON PACO
~ TOWN HOTEL ~

Posada Herrera 1, 33500 Llanes, Asturias
TEL (98) 5400150 **FAX** (98) 5402681

The most startling feature of this hotel is the restaurant, which occupies the huge arched and vaulted hall of the original 17thC palace that forms the basis of the present-day building. It is truly impressive, with stone pilasters, an ancient polished wood floor and splendid chandeliers, and a mezzanine area from where you can survey the other diners. Local specialities include a spiny lobster which is caught in pots off the coast. Double doors lead out on to the terrace which is above the level of the pavement, beneath pollarded plane trees and shrubs sheltering the tables from the sun and the passers-by. From here you can admire the handsome stone façade of the palace as you take your coffee or aperitif.

The rest of the the hotel is rather dull in comparison, and showing signs of wear, but many of the old-fashioned bedrooms look out over the quiet square or the back of the building away from the traffic. The town itself is full of bustle and interesting shops, as well as the remains of its defensive walls and castle. There are plenty of beaches nearby and the grand Picos de Europa with their rivers and mountains are within easy reach.

~

Nearby Monasterio de S. Antolin (10 km); Peña Tú (5 km) – megalith with engravings.
Location in heart of town; with some car parking
Meals breakfast, lunch, dinner
Prices rooms ⓔⓔ; breakfast P; meals ⓔⓔ
Rooms 38 double, 36 with bath, 2 with shower; 4 single with shower; all rooms have central heating, phone, TV
Facilities dining-room, sitting-room, bar
Credit cards AE, DC, MC, V
Children accepted
Disabled lift/elevator; some ground-floor rooms
Pets not accepted
Closed 1 Oct to 1 Jun
Manager Alfredo Sanpedro

ASTURIAS

BARRO, LLANES

Kaype

~ Beach hotel ~

Playa de Barro s/n, 33500, Llanes, Asturias
Tel (98) 5400904 **Fax** (98) 5400418

Situated on the beautiful sandy Barro beach, this is a functional and friendly place for a seaside or mountain walking holiday: the Picos de Europa are not far inland. All the rooms have a view of either the sea or the mountains. A semi-covered terrace extends from the dining area, an agreeable place in which to chat or to read on days when there is no orbayu, the persistent but essential rain from the north. Unusually, the hotel has its own shellfish nurseries which supply its restaurant.

Obliging and generous, the staff have managed to build up a loyal clientele that returns year after year to the same rooms.

~

Nearby Torimbia beach (2 km); Llanes (6 km); Picos de Europa and Covadonga National Park (42 km).
Location on the beach; car parking
Meals breakfast, lunch, dinner
Prices rooms €€; breakfast €; meals €€
Rooms 48 double, all with bath; all rooms have central heating, telephone
Facilities sitting-room, bar, dining-room; terrace
Credit cards AE, DC, MC, V
Children welcome **Disabled** all rooms equipped; lift/elevator
Pets not accepted **Closed** Oct to Apr **Manager** José Manuel González

LLANES

Paraíso

~ Town hotel ~

Pidal, 2, 33500, Llanes, Asturias
Tel (98) 5401971 **Fax** (98) 5402590

This large house with prominent tiers of bay windows was tastefully renovated a few years ago as a hotel-cum-summer apartment block for families. The interior decoration, it has to be said, with its white marbles, mahogany walls and antique furniture, seems a little kitsch and decadent. Another shortcoming is noise at night from the street below. From your bedroom an intercom links you directly to a valet waiting to attend your every need: whether it be a snack, a baby-sitter or today's paper, you only have to ask. A recent inspector thought the bedrooms well-equipped but uninspiring. 'Not as much charm as we would wish, but good value for families and those who want to be close the the beach and shops.'

~

Nearby the idol of Peña-Tú; Vidiago (5 km); Toró beach (1 km).
Location in the main street of the town, next to the harbour; garage nearby
Meals breakfast
Prices rooms €€-€€€; breakfast €
Rooms 22 double, 12 suites, all with bath; all rooms have air conditioning, telephone, minibar, radio, TV (satellite), safe **Facilities** sitting-room, cafeteria
Credit cards AE, DC, MC, V **Children** welcome
Disabled no special facilities; lift/elevator **Pets** not accepted
Closed Nov to Mar **Proprietor** Antonio Ampudia

ASTURIAS

FIGUERAS DEL MAR

PALACETE PEÑALBA
~ TOWN HOTEL ~

El Cotarelo s/n, 33794, Figueras, Asturias
TEL (98) 5636125 **FAX** (98) 5636247

This extraordinary house was built in 1912 by a disciple of the celebrated Spanish architect Antonio Gaudí. Everything about it – the curved sweep of the entrance steps, the ovals of the balconies, the glazed and tiled atrium, the twin towers with their delicate plasterwork, the arched alcoves in the bedrooms – is redolent of the early Art Nouveau movement which took root in Europe at this time. Much of the original furniture and internal decoration, such as the tapestries, has been preserved, and the whole edifice has been declared a National Artistic Monument. In fact, the atmosphere does rather resemble that of a museum – beware the elegant but delicate chairs in the sitting-room. This is not a place to bring unruly children, but if you enjoy the absurdities of this particular era you will come anyway.

The town of Figueras del Mar has been by-passed by the new bridge over the Ria de Ribadeo, but it is busy with fishing and shipbuilding. The hotel's owners also run a restaurant on the waterfront, and both establishments have a reputation in the area for interesting cuisine – specializing, needless to say, in seafood.

~

Nearby Castropol (5 km); beach and lighthouse at Tapia de Casariego (10 km).
Location at top of town above port; with grounds and car parking
Meals breakfast
Prices rooms €€-€€€; breakfast P
Rooms 12 double, 2 suites, all with bath; all rooms have central heating, radio, TV, minibar, phone, safe
Facilities dining-room, sitting-room, bar
Credit cards AE, V
Children welcome
Disabled access difficult
Pets not accepted
Closed never
Proprietor Avelino Gutierrez

ASTURIAS

RIBADESELLA

HOTEL RIBADESELLA PLAYA

～ SEASIDE HOTEL ～

Ricardo Cangas, 3, 33560, Ribadesella, Asturias
TEL (98) 5860715 **FAX** (98) 5860220

Ribadesella has long been quite a stylish resort, popular with holiday-makers attracted by the port and the estuary of the river Sella, with its sandy beaches and spectacular scenery. The Hotel Ribadesella Playa, converted from one of the many old family villas which line the bay, across the river from the main town, has recently been sensitively modernized.

The hotel is right on the beach, beside a grassed promenade, free of traffic, and many of the bedrooms – smartly done up with traditional-style modern furniture – have long windows and balconies with views over the water. The restaurant is in the lower part of the house, cool and airy, with stone floors and sympathetic wooden furniture. The *carte* is long and varied, with plenty of fresh fish dishes, and there is also a menu of the day if you prefer your selection made for you.

The hotel has no pretensions to luxury, but combines comfortable accommodation with a relaxed and informal atmosphere. A happy choice for a beach holiday, with the added advantage for many visitors of the nearby town and the mountains with their walks, caves and birdlife.

～

Nearby Caves of Tito Bustillo (5 km); Mirador de la Reina (45 km).
Location in quiet residential beach area on W side of town; car parking in courtyard
Meals breakfast, lunch, dinner
Prices rooms €€; breakfast P; meals €€
Rooms 16 double, 1 single, all with bath; all rooms have central heating, phone, TV
Facilities dining-room, 2 sitting-rooms
Credit cards AE, DC, MC, V
Children accepted
Disabled no special facilities
Pets not accepted
Closed never
Manager José Luis García

ASTURIAS

BESNES

LA TAHONA
~ MOUNTAIN HOTEL ~

33578, Besnes-Alles, Asturias
TEL & FAX (98) 5415749

DRIVING FROM PANES UP into the Picos de Europa, you follow the course of the Río Cares, up through a deep and dramatic gorge which winds on towards some of the most stupendous views to be found in these mountains. La Tahona is tucked away behind the tiny village of Besnes, at the end of a cobbled track, beside a stream which runs down through beech woods. It is a peaceful and simple base for walking, horseriding, down-river canoeing or mountain-biking.

The bar by the entrance hall is used by a few local farmers who drop in for a quiet coffee and brandy on their way up and down the valley; beyond is the rustic restaurant, all bare stone, exposed beams, whitewashed rough plaster and red tiles. Bedrooms are similarly simple, but stylish.

The stream runs past the restaurant, the terrace and the windows of the bedrooms – the soothing sound of water and birdsong will be your only distractions while contemplating the choice between salmon with cider, trout from the river or Asturian hotpot. 'A fabulous little place'; 'good value'; 'excellent (huge) packed lunches', says a recent reporter. In marked contrast, another complains of being woken by creaking floorboards; of poor lighting; and of an 'unstylish' bedroom. Further reports especially welcome.

~

NEARBY El Buxu – prehistoric cave paintings (30 km); viewpoint at Las Estazadas (8 km).
LOCATION in quiet wooded valley, off C6312 10 km W of Panes; with garden and car parking
Meals breakfast, lunch, dinner
PRICES rooms €€; breakfast €; meals €€
ROOMS 18 double, one family room, all with bath; all rooms have central heating, TV, phone **FACILITIES** dining-room, sitting-room; horse-riding, mountain bikes, fishing, canoeing **CREDIT CARDS** MC, V **CHILDREN** welcome; play-room; special menus **DISABLED** access easy; some ground-floor rooms **PETS** not accepted **CLOSED** never **MANAGERS** Lorenzo and Sarah Nilsson

ASTURIAS

PONGA

La Casona de Mestas

~ Mountain hotel ~

Las Mestas 33557, Ponga, Asturias
Tel (98) 5843055 **Fax** (98) 5843092

To reach this mountain hideaway you follow the sinuous course of the Ponga river to the regional capital of San Juan de Beleño, passing below sheer rocky hillsides and climbing over beautiful passes. The hotel – another Rural Tourism Centre – is at the heart of some of the most spectacular walking country you could hope to find anywhere, with several well known routes starting at the Casona itself. The main building has been converted from an old house with overhanging, Alpine-style roofs, and the restaurant area is a sympathetic modern, wooden glass-sided extension looking out on to fabulous views of the surrounding peaks.

~

Nearby Desfiladero de los Beyos (25 km); thermal baths .
Location in mountainous countryside near village, about 30 km S of Cangas de Onis; with car parking
Meals breakfast, lunch, dinner
Prices rooms €€; breakfast €; meals €€
Rooms 6 double, 6 single all with bath; all rooms have central heating
Facilities dining-room, cafeteria, TV room
Credit cards V
Children accepted **Disabled** no special facilities **Pets** not accepted
Closed mid-Jan to mid- Feb **Manager** Georges Gonzalez

TARAMUNDI

La Rectoral

~ Mountain hotel ~

33775, Taramundi, Asturias
Tel (98) 5646767 **Fax** (98) 5646777

This was the first of the Rural Tourism hotels to be encouraged by the government of Asturias – a lovely old 18thC stone house converted into simple but comfortable accommodation reflecting the architectural, decorative and gastronomic traditions of the region. It is on the western side of Asturias, on the border with Lugo, in the remote hilly country of Los Oscos. The Rectoral looks out over unspoiled countryside which is still quietly tilled using locally made tools. Six of the bedrooms have their own lounge and private terrace, sharing the peaceful view with the hotel's patio.

~

Nearby Monastery, Villanueva de Oscos (20 km).
Location on a hill, going up from the main square of the village, in front of the town hall; garden, covered car parking
Meals breakfast, lunch, dinner
Prices rooms €€€-€€€€; breakfast €; meals €€ **Rooms** 18 double, all with bath; all rooms have central heating, air-conditioning, phone, TV, radio, minibar **Facilities** dining-room, sitting-rooms, TV room, cafeteria, sauna, gymnasium **Credit cards** AE, MC, V **Children** accepted **Disabled** no special facilities **Pets** not accepted **Closed** never **Manager** Jesus Manuel Mier

ASTURIAS

AMANDI, VILLAVICIOSA

LA CASONA DE AMANDI
~ COUNTRY HOUSE HOTEL ~

Amandi, 33300, Villaviciosa, Asturias
TEL (98) 5890130 **FAX** (98) 5890129

RODRIGO FERNANDEZ AND HIS WIFE María Isabel Armero bought this old colonial mansion on the outskirts of Villaviciosa with the idea of turning it into a secluded country hotel in the heart of the magnificent Asturias. Close by is Ría de Villaviciosa, famous for its rich birdlife.

The proprietors' good taste, and former profession as antique dealers, is reflected in every corner: from the façade with traditional bay windows, to the Elizabethan furniture and the French garden full of hydrangeas and magnolias. This is a peaceful retreat, very much a village house, smelling of wood and mown grass.

The rooms preserve their old fittings: there are authentic washbasins and shaving bowls in some of the bathrooms. Elsewhere there are similar details: grandmother's pianola, for instance, in the sitting room. On the other hand, there is no lack of modern comfort.

The welcome is sincere and personal; Rodrigo and María live on the premises. An outstanding base from which to make forays into 'Green Spain'.

~

NEARBY Ría de Villaviciosa (5 km); Rodiles beach (10 km); Tazones fishing harbour (10 km).
LOCATION on a narrow lane, 1 km from Villaviciosa; with garden and car parking
MEALS breakfast
PRICES rooms €€€; breakfast €
ROOMS 8 double, 1 single, all with bath; all rooms have central heating, telephone, TV
FACILITIES sitting-room/library
CREDIT CARDS MC, V
CHILDREN welcome **DISABLED** access difficult **PETS** not accepted
CLOSED never
PROPRIETORS Rodrigo Fernández and María Isabel Armero

ASTURIAS

COLLIA ARRIONDAS

POSADA DEL VALLE
~ MOUNTAIN HOTEL ~

33549 Collia Arriondas, Asturias
TEL (985) 841 157 **FAX** (985) 841 559
E-MAIL hotel@posadadelvalle.com

Nigel Burch and his wife Joanne opened in 1997 after a mid-life change of direction: he had had a successful career in horticulture, moving here from a big farm in southern Spain. Out of a late 19th-C 'priest's farmhouse', built on a rock outcrop with a stunning views over the Picos, they have carved a cosy but comfortable family hotel. Its strongest point is the friendly family atmosphere: you'll get a genuinely personal welcome here, from people who are fresh to the business, together with all the advice you need about exploring the area. It's a great base for the Picos de Europa, the Ponga Mountain Range, the Sueve Reserve, the coastline of Eastern Asturias and the River Sella. Walking, surfing, mountain biking, canoeing, fishing and more, are within reach.

The decoration is relatively simple and pleasing, making the most of the building's original features, including thick walls and exposed stonework. Picture windows give the dining-room (good home cooking) a wonderful outlook over a lush green valley rising to a limestone peak. Bedrooms are simple but comfortable, in rustic style, with pretty, well-chosen fabrics. A welcome addition to the guide in an area short of our sort of hotel. No smoking allowed in the house.

~

Nearby outdoor pursuits
Location signposted from the AS-260 on right 1 km (0.5 mile) N out of Arriondas; in own large gardens with car parking
Meals breakfast, dinner
Price €€
Rooms 8 double, all with bathroom
Facilities sitting-room, dining-room, bar, garden
Credit cards MC V
Children over 8 years **Disabled** Not suitable **Pets** Not accepted
Closed 16 Oct-14 Mar
Proprietors Nigel and Joanne Burch

ASTURIAS

VILLANUEVA-CANGAS DE ONIS

PARADOR DE CANGAS DE ONIS
~ COUNTRY HOTEL ~

3500 Villanueva-Cangas de Onis, Asturias
TEL (98) 584 9402 FAX (98) 584 9520
E-MAIL cangas@parador.es

This relatively new parador scores impressively on most of our selection criteria. The building was formerly the monastery of San Pedro de Villanueva, probably founded in the 12th century, and like many a monastery it has a wonderful setting: in this case the banks of the River Sella, on the edge of the remarkable limestone scenery of the Picos de Europa. The interior centres around a magnificent courtyard and cloisters; a small church is attached, still open for services, with some well-preserved carved figures and painted ceilings. The restaurant and 64 bedrooms are housed in a new building connected to the original by a glass corridor. Our inspector describes the food as interesting, with the emphasis on Astrias, both on the menu and the wine list; it's served by waitresses in local costume. Staff are 'particularly welcoming and friendly.'

The nearby small town of Cangas de Onis is attractive, with plenty of shops and restaurants. In short, a gem.

~

Nearby Covadonga, historic battlefield; Picos de Europa
Location 21/2 km from centre; not easy to find – ask for directions; with own extensive car parking
Meals breakfast, lunch, dinner
Price €€€
Rooms 64 doubles, all with heating, air-conditioning
Facilities garden, swimming-pool, gym, solarium, golf course planned
Credit cards AE DC MC V
Children welcome; no charge in medium and low season if sharing room with parents; special menu
Disabled special ground-floor room, suitable elevator
Pets not accepted
Closed never
Manager Cesar Alvarez

PONTEVEDRA

CAMBADOS

PT DEL ALBARIÑO

～ MANSION PARADOR ～

Paseo de Cervantes s/n, 36630, Cambados, Pontevedra
TEL (986) 542250 **FAX** (986) 542068

Cambados is a happy little holiday town which is at its best in the sum-mer months, a judgement equally applicable to the Parador, which can be bleak and cold in winter (like any hotel in an abandoned seaside town in the off-season).

The hotel is built around a courtyard garden with palm trees and a fountain, and for anyone in vacation mood it offers cool and relaxed accommodation, right beside the protected estuary of the Ría de Arousa, with its islands and wooded banks. The water here is not as clean as Atlantic water would be, but this does not seem to deter local bathers.

There are several interesting bars and restaurants in the town with its peaceful, shady squares and long tree-lined promenade if you decide not to eat in the rather predictable Parador dining-room. Inevitably the spe-cialities of this area are fish and shellfish, but most menus offer meat dishes too. The wines of the west coast can be delicious, particularly some of the young green wines, known locally as joven – the Parador itself is named after a wine brought to the area by Benedictine monks in the twelfth century.

～

Nearby Plaza de Fefiñanes; Monastery of Armenteira (10 km);
island of La Toja (10 km).
Location in lovely gardens at north end of promenade; with car parking
Meals breakfast, lunch, dinner
Prices rooms ⓔⓔⓔ-ⓔⓔⓔⓔ; breakfast ⓔ; dinner ⓔⓔ
Rooms 51 double, 12 single, all with bath; all rooms have central heating, phone
TV, safe
Facilities dining-room, sitting-room, bar, swimming-pool
Credit cards AE, DC, MC, V
Children welcome **Disabled** some ground-floor rooms **Pets** not accepted
Closed never
Manager Carlos Herrero

PONTEVEDRA

VILLAGARCIA DE AROSA

HOTEL PAZO O'RIAL

~ COUNTRY HOTEL ~

El Rial No 1, 36600, Villagarcía de Arosa, Pontevedra
TEL (986) 507011 **FAX** (986) 501676

The road here runs along beside the Ría de Arosa as it opens out towards the sea, not quite the open Atlantic, but nevertheless a holiday area for many Spanish visitors as well as northern Europeans.

This lovely old manor house is set back from the coast in its own gardens and has been beautifully converted, making full use of all the usual traditional effects – wooden beams, tiled floors and bare stone walls. The whole effect is softened with deep cushioned sofas, lacy curtains and woollen rugs. The service has been criticised as slack but there is nothing amiss with the housekeeping, the gardening or the cleanliness of the pool, which is surrounded by a protective hedge on one side and lovely views over the countryside on the other.

This is another area famous for its seafood – the bays around here are packed with fish and shellfish farms, and every inlet seems to have its little fleet of fishing boats to win a share of the harvest. The menu of the hotel reflects this, with the ubiquitous grilled prawns coming high on the list along with huge mussels in a thick tomato sauce. We're retaining this hotel for one more edition despite a negative report on the food and the bedrooms ('dull'). Further opinions welcome.

~

Nearby Vista Alegre Convent; Mirador de Lobeira (5 km).
Location near sea, set back from road; with car parking
Meals breakfast, lunch, dinner
Prices rooms €€; breakfast €; meals €€
Rooms 49 double, 6 single, 4 suites, one family room; all with bath; all rooms have central heating, phone, TV
Facilities dining-room, sitting-room, bar
Credit cards AE, DC, MC, V
Children welcome **Disabled** access easy; ground-floor rooms; lift/elevator
Pets not accepted **Closed** never
Manager Julio Mondragón

PONTEVEDRA

VILLALONGA

HOTEL PAZO EL REVEL
～ COUNTRY HOTEL ～

Camino de la Iglesia s/n, 36990, Villalonga, Pontevedra
TEL (986) 743000 **FAX** (986) 743390

Back from the coast road and the small town of Villalonga, up a lane which leads to walks in the hills, a little church and the local cemetery, this lovely 17thC pazo is the family home of Luis Ansorena Garret, an aristocratic gentleman who has run this hotel along his own lines since the 1960s.

The creeper-covered façade has no noticeboard or sign to give the hotel away. You park across the lane and help will be at hand to carry your bags through the archway to the courtyard and your neat, tiled room. Swallows nest in the age-old beams and eaves of the house and verandas, while quiet men rake the gravel and tend the beautiful formal gardens and lawns.

In the heat of summer, nothing could be more calming than to take your iced fino to the colonnaded terrace overlooking the trees and flowers and to sit in a padded wicker armchair for an hour or so before dinner. The dining-room is quite informal and – please note – is open only at the height of the season; but lazy breakfasts can be enjoyed into the late morning, making the most of the excellent fresh coffee and newly baked rolls, croissants and sweet cakes.

～

Nearby Cambados – pazos and restaurants (10 km); beaches at San Vicente do Mar (5 km).
Location a short way up hill overlooking town; with gardens and car parking
Meals breakfast, lunch, dinner
Prices rooms €€-€€€; breakfast €; meals €€
Rooms 20 double, 2 single, all with bath; all rooms have central heating, phone
Facilities dining-room,
sitting-room, bar, terrace; tennis court, swimming-pool
Credit cards MC, V
Children tolerated **Disabled** access difficult **Pets** not accepted **Closed** Oct to May
Proprietor Luis Ansorena

PONTEVEDRA

PONTEVEDRA

PT CASA DEL BARON
⟶ Historic Parador ⟵

Calle Maceda s/n,36002, Pontevedra
Tel (986) **Fax** (986) 852195

The approach to Pontevedra is not promising: the roads are extremely busy and smoke belches from a cement works. But, as so often in Spain, as soon as you turn into the old town, you are suddenly immersed in another world, with cobbled streets and shutters, balconies and stone façades which tell of a different way of life.

The Parador is at the heart of Pontevedra's old town, and is one of the most captivating of the chain, occupying a beautiful old pazo which has been the home of many grandees. It is not imposing, but rather elegant, with plenty of antiques which are meant to be used rather than just admired, giving you the feeling that this is a place where you should know how to behave –the suites in the sitting-rooms are covered in apricot-coloured suede, for example.

The dining-room is hung with tapestries and chandeliers, gilt mirrors and paintings, and overlooks the terraced garden with its fountain and rosebeds. As with many of the Paradores there are regional dishes on the menu and at the Casa del Barón this may include lamprea (lamprey), which can be very rich and is something of an acquired taste.

⟶

Nearby Museo Provincial; Mirador de Coto Redondo (15 km).
Location on cobbled street in heart of old town; with garden and car parking in courtyard
Meals breakfast, lunch, dinner
Prices rooms €€-€€€€ breakfast €; dinner €€
Rooms 44 double, 3 single, all with bath; all rooms have central heating, phone, TV, hairdrier, minibar, safe
Facilities dining-room, 2 sitting-rooms, bar, conference room
Credit cards AE, DC, MC, V
Children welcome **Disabled** lift/elevator **Pets** not accepted
Closed never
Manager José Basso

ORENSE

VERÍN

PT MONTERREY
~ MODERN HILLTOP PARADOR ~

32600, Verín, Orense
TEL (988) 410075 **FAX** (988) 412017

The 'Monterrey' Parador is named after the dramatic castle which occupies a neighbouring hilltop, and which you can see for many miles before you reach the town of Verín. Parts of the castle church date back to the 13th century and there are towers from the 16th and 17th centuries. The whole complex was abandoned around a hundred years ago but the fortifications are now undergoing restoration.

In contrast, the Parador is a relatively recent construction, though it has been built in local stone with concessions to regional architectural style and it sits happily on its own hilltop surrounded by trees and lawns. As Paradores go it is undistinguished and is scarcely a place to spend the whole of your holidays, but the swimming-pool, the breezy setting and the nearby sights make it worthy of a short stopover.

The old town of Verín itself is quiet and picturesque, and the valley of the Támega river which runs off north from here is lined with vineyards. Wines from nearby which appear on the Parador list and which are worth trying include the lovely fruity whites from Ribeiro.

~

Nearby Mineral water spas at Sousas, Cabreiroa and Villaza, and bottling factory at Fontenova (5 km).
Location on hill above town; with garden and car parking
Meals breakfast, lunch, dinner
Prices rooms €€€-€€€€; breakfast €; meals €€
Rooms rooms 22 double, one single, all with bath; all rooms have central heating, phone, TV, minibar
Facilities dining-room, sitting-room, bar, terrace; swimming-pool
Credit cards AE, DC, MC, V
Children accepted
Disabled some ground-floor bedrooms
Pets not accepted
Closed never
Manager Jesús Santamaría

ORENSE

PUEBLA DE TRIVES

PAZO CASA GRANDE
~ TOWN HOTEL ~

Marqués de Trives 17, 32780, Poboa de Trives, Orense
TEL & FAX (988)332066

Pazo Casa Grande is a noble 18thC stone mansion clustered around a solid central tower, crowned by a coat of arms showing a knight on horseback killing a dragon. For many years the house lay in a state of disrepair until the Alvarez family decided to renovate it in the late 1980s and open it as a pousada, or little hotel.

From the outside, the Casa Grande appears to be an imposing, aristocratic residence; but inside its thick walls all is elegant, cosy and welcoming. It is furnished and decorated with antiques and Limoges ceramics, and original watercolours adorn the walls. The 18thC piano is a decoration: Doña Adelaida now prefers a modern instrument. Like any self-respecting big house, Pazo Casa Grande has its own chapel which every year, on the feast of Corpus Christi, is decorated with a carpet of flowers.

Outside, there is a delightful garden with fruit trees and a copse of chestnuts. This is a popular base from which to follow the Route of the Monasteries (Ribera Sagrada), also the Romanesque Route, and in winter for skiing.

~

Nearby Montefurado reservoir (6 km); Montaña Manzaneda ski resort (16 km); San Esteban de Ribas de Sil Monastery and gorges of the River Sil (60 km).
Location in a main street of the town; garden and car parking
Meals breakfast
Prices rooms €€; breakfast €
Rooms 7 double, with bath; all rooms have central heating, TV
Facilities dining-room, TV room, chapel
Credit cards AE, DC, MC, V
Children welcome; play area
Disabled access difficult
Pets accepted, outside the house; kennels (1km)
Closed never
Proprietor Adelaida Alvarez

LEON

HOSTAL EL PALACIO
~ TOWN HOTEL ~

Calle Palacio 3, 24200, Valencia de Don Juan, León
TEL & FAX (987) 750474

For 25 years the Eguens ran this welcoming but little-known hotel which specializes in excellent, wholesome home cooking and cider. Though it has recently had a change of owner we are still happy to recommend it; however, reports will be especially welcome.

Austrian-born José Manuel Eguen knew practically everything there is to know about the bottle. In the old stables at the back he built a *sidrería* – a bar – out of black wood seasoned with the smell of cider. It is also a fascinating folk museum; on the walls you will find a prehistoric one-way telephone and an ancient precursor of the Thermos flask.

The house is probably the oldest in the village, certainly the only one bearing a coat of arms. King Felipe III is supposed to have stopped off here once upon a time and seduced the mistress of the house; there is a framed document in the hall to prove it.

The patio – shaded by Virginia creeper and vines – has an old cart in one corner, painted bright red and green, and a five-foot-long blacksmith's bellows in another. A cool and attractive alternative to the dining-room and sitting-room, it is looked down upon by a wide iron-railinged balcony on the first floor: both are pleasant places to sit. The rooms are light, cheerful and spotlessly clean.

~

Nearby Castle; León (30 km); San Miguel de Escalada (45 km).
Location in centre of town; car parking in street
Meals breakfast, lunch, dinner
Prices rooms €-€€(half-price for children); breakfast €; dinner €
Rooms 7 double, 3 single, all with bath; all rooms have TV
Facilities dining-room, sitting-room, bar, patio
Credit cards not accepted
Children welcome **Disabled** access difficult
Pets not accepted
Closed 1Oct to 1May
Proprietor Monica Gonzalez

LEON

VALENCIA DE DON JUAN

HOTEL VILLEGAS II
∽ TOWN HOTEL ∽

Calle Palacio 17, 24200, Valencia de Don Juan, León
TEL (987) 750161

Villegas II looks and sometimes feels more like a private house in its own grounds than a hotel. You might even drive past it, as we did, without noticing the blue hotel plaque by the door. From its external appearance you would expect the hotel to be pleasant and home-like inside, and it does not disappoint. The entrance hall is dominated by blue tiles and light wrought iron, and lit by a stained glass skylight. Neo-Arabic arches lead to the bar, dining-room and a small lounge.

All of the bedrooms give on to the garden. They have been decorated with some flair; the bedspreads and curtains are white-and-blue flowered, much of the furniture is of light wood and the doors and door-frames are of stripped pine. An outbuilding has been added recently to provide an extra public room and bedrooms.

Outside, there is a fringe of garden all round the building, which takes in a swimming-pool and an outdoor dining-terrace.

This hotel is everything that the Palacio (see separate entry) over the road is not. Here you can choose between two facing hotels – both charming in different ways. (Villegas I, by the way, is something else again: a modern multi-storey block down the road.)

∽

Nearby Castle (short walk); León (30 km); San Miguel de Escalada (45 km); Astorga (55 km).
Location in centre of town; with garden and car parking
Meals breakfast, lunch, dinner
Prices rooms €€; breakfast €; lunch €€, dinner €€
Rooms 14 double, one family room, all with bath; all rooms have central heating, TV
Facilities dining-room, sitting-room, bar, terrace; swimming-pool
Credit cards AE, DC, MC, V
Children welcome; garden play area **Disabled** access difficult
Pets not accepted **Closed** Dec to Feb **Proprietor** Felisa Garcia

LEON

ASTORGA

HOTEL GAUDI

~ TOWN HOTEL ~

Plaza Eduardo de Castro 6, 24700, Astorga, León
TEL (987) 615654 **FAX** (987) 615040

The Hotel Gaudí is right in the middle of Astorga, on the main square which has seen the meeting of Roman roads, the passing of pilgrims on their way to Santiago, and the building of the extraordinary Episcopal Palace. The Hotel takes its name from the Barcelona architect, Antonio Gaudí, who built this wildly decorated pastiche of a Gothic palace in 1889. It now houses a museum about the pilgrim ways to Santiago de Compostela.

This stylish, modern hotel offers comforts far removed from the sort of conditions those earlier travellers would have encountered. The elegant restaurant, with its marble floor, chandeliers and panelled walls, overlooks the square – as does the bar area, which serves excellent tapas. Many of the bedrooms have balconies, their shutters opening on to views of the huge and complicated cathedral, with its flying buttresses and carvings, the Gaudí palace and the surrounding terracotta roofs above narrow, cobbled lanes. They are individually furnished and most are carpeted, which makes a pleasantly soft change after the bare boards and marble floors of so many Spanish hotels.

The quiet square is mostly used as a car park and is bordered by trees, shrubs and flowers, cafés and shops.

~

Nearby León (40 km).
Location in main square near cathedral and Gaudí palace; with car parking in square
Meals breakfast, lunch, dinner
Prices rooms €€-€€€€; breakfast €; meals €€
Rooms 35 double, 3 suites, all with bath; all rooms have central heating, phone, TV, radio
Facilities dining-room, sitting-room, bar
Credit cards AE, DC, MC, V **Children** accepted **Disabled** access difficult
Pets not accepted **Closed** never **Proprietor** Gaspar Ramos

CANTABRIA

COSGAYA

HOTEL DEL OSO
~ MOUNTAIN HOTEL ~

39539, Cosgaya, Cantabria
TEL (942) 733018 **FAX** (942) 733036

You will already have come through some exceptional scenery to reach Cosgaya, climbing steadily all the way from the coast, and once you arrive you are surrounded by peaks, many snow- covered until early summer.

A small bridge over a clear mountain stream takes you into the forecourt of this stone-built hotel, with its wooden balconies, arched veranda and overflowing flowerpots. The public rooms are cool and dark in the summer heat, but cosy and welcoming in the winter, with log fires in the sitting-room. Although the hotel has only recently been built, it is traditional in style with plenty of workmanship to admire, in wood, terracotta tiling and bare stonework. The restaurant, too, makes use of regional specialities – fresh river trout, interesting local cheeses and regional spirits.

There is always the chance of getting snowed in when staying in this area, so bring plenty of books – it has been known to happen in June, though at that time of year you are more likely to be lazing around their pool, playing tennis or off hiking in the hills. They are used to British visitors here, and good English is spoken at the desk.

~

Nearby Cable-car at Fuente De (10 km) to 1800 m.
Location by stream in mountains; with garden and car parking
Meals breakfast, lunch, dinner
Prices rooms €€; breakfast €; dinner €€
Rooms 32 double, 4 single, all with bath; all rooms have central heating, phone, TV
Facilities dining-room, 3 sitting-rooms, bar; swimming-pool, tennis court
Credit cards DC, MC, V
Children welcome
Disabled access difficult
Pets not accepted
Closed 15 Jan to 15 Feb
Proprietor Severo Rivas

CANTABRIA

SANTILLANA DEL MAR

PT GIL BLAS
~ Historic Parador ~

Plaza Ramón Pelayo 11, 39330, Santillana del Mar, Cantabria
Tel (942) 818000 **Fax** (942) 818391

On a fleeting visit, Santillana can seem like an overpopulated film set, but if you stay overnight you will have opportunity and time to take in the essence of the place. The Parador Gil Blas – one of the most captivating of the Paradores – is without doubt the place to stay if you have the choice.

Gil Blas was the fictional hero of a story by the French writer Lesage, a fact seemingly unconnected with the house itself, which was the country home of the Barreda Bracho family, built in the 15th and 16th centuries. The worn stone, the lovely terracotta roof tiles, the delightful courtyard garden and the cobbled entrance hall are all in harmony with the medieval atmosphere of the village.

There are two parts to this Parador – the original fine old manor house right in the centre of Santillana del Mar, and the new annexe across the square. It would not be a complete disaster if you ended up with a new room, but the character of Gil Blas is something special and the rooms are exceptional; many have long windows and balconies but the ones overlooking the garden are probably the most pleasant.

~

Nearby Villas House, Calle de Santo Domingo; Velarde Tower, Plaza de Las Arenas; Altamira cave exhibition (5 km).
Location on main square in heart of village; with garden and garage
Meals breakfast, lunch, dinner
Prices rooms €€-€€€€€; breakfast €; meals €€
Rooms 51 double, 4 single; all rooms have central heating, phone, TV, minibar, safe **Facilities** dining-room, 3 sitting-rooms, breakfast room, sauna, bar, conference room
Credit cards AE, DC, MC, V
Children accepted **Disabled** no special facilities **Pets** not accepted
Closed never
Manager Joachim Blanelles

CANTABRIA

SANTILLANA DEL MAR

HOTEL ALTAMIRA

~ VILLAGE HOTEL ~

Cantón 1, 39330, Santillana del Mar, Cantabria
TEL (942) 818025 **FAX** (942) 840136

If you want to be right in the heart of the old village of Santillana del Mar, in an old house which has retained much of its character whilst offering full facilities, but you have had enough of Paradores, then the Hotel Altamira will probably suit you.

The hotel was extended to take in the house next door, and has a large courtyard garden at the back which doubles as a terrace for outside dining or drinking when the weather is right. The place has a comfortable air of antiquity, with old chests, chairs, paintings and mirrors dotted around, but is not at all like a museum.

The restaurant is in country style, with red and white cloths and tiled floors, the breakfast room quiet, dark and green, under lovely stone arches. The wooden stairs – pleasantly creaky, with nicely old-fashioned flowered carpet – lead from the stone-flagged entrance hall up to the sitting-rooms and bedrooms which are found off at interesting angles and on different levels. The bedrooms themselves are furnished in keeping with the atmosphere of the house, with its polished wood floors, beams and, in places, bare stone walls.

~

Nearby Villas House, Calle de Santo Domingo; Velarde Tower, Plaza de Las Arenas; Altamira cave exhibition (5 km).
Location in old village, on road to church; no private car parking, but municipal car park nearby
Meals breakfast, lunch, dinner
Prices rooms €€-€€€; breakfast P; meals PP
Rooms 19 double, 5 single, 2 suites, 6 family rooms, all with bath; all rooms have central heating, phone, TV, hairdrier
Facilities 2 dining-rooms, 1 sitting-room, bar, terrace, café
Credit cards AE, DC, MC, V
Children accepted **Disabled** access difficult **Pets** not accepted
Closed 24 Dec and 31 Jan **Manager** David Oceja

CANTABRIA

SANTILLANA DEL MAR

LOS INFANTES

～ VILLAGE HOTEL ～

Avenida Le Dorat 1, 39330, Santillana del Mar, Cantabria
TEL (942) 818100 **FAX** (942) 840103

The Hotel Los Infantes, set slightly back from the main road, just outside the village of Santillana del Mar, has been built around a lovely old 18thC stone country house. Entering the hall from the terrace through a decorated stone archway you can sense the grandeur of the old ways of life. There are huge carved chests on stone floors, wrought iron chandeliers hanging from high ceilings with massive wooden beams, and an impressive collection of antique clocks. The bar is in the lobby area, and you can sink into a deep leather armchair and soak up the atmosphere here or take your drink out into the sheltered garden. The upstairs sitting-room also has leather armchairs, as well as more formal reproduction furniture.

The restaurant is modern and unfussy, in café style. Some of the bedrooms are rather undistinguished, with small bathrooms; others are individually furnished with antique bed-heads, paintings on the walls, white handwoven bedspreads, comfortable chairs, carpets, balconies and large, immaculate bathrooms. A few metres from the hotel is a recent annexe offering 20 more bedrooms.

～

Nearby sights of Santillana del Mar; Altamira cave exhibition (1.5 km).
Location on main road past village, near Diocesano Museum; parking for 20 cars
Meals breakfast, lunch, dinner
Prices rooms €€-€€€€; breakfast €; meals €€
Rooms 25 double, 3 single, 2 suites, all with bath; all rooms have central heating, phone, TV
Facilities dining-room, sitting-room
Credit cards AE, DC, MC, V
Children accepted
Disabled ground-floor rooms
Pets by arrangement only
Closed Oct to Apr
Proprietor Mesones Gómez

CANTABRIA

SANTILLANA DEL MAR

POSADA SANTA JULIANA

~ VILLAGE INN WITH ROOMS ~

Carrera 19, 39330, Santillana del Mar, Cantabria.
TEL (942) 840106 **FAX** (942) 840170

ALTHOUGH THE BEDROOMS are unpromisingly located above a souvenir shop, with their chestnut floors and oak beams, they do share some of Santillana's undiluted medieval atmosphere – especially the two in the attic.

There are no public rooms and meals are served in the bar across the street, Bodegón El Noble, where you will find the genial owner, Sr Morquilles.

The framed letter and royal shield on the souvenir shop wall explain why animals are not accepted in the posada: the Queen of Spain's dogs once stayed here but they scratched the doors.

~

Nearby sights of Santillana del Mar; Altamira caves (2km).
Location in one of the main streets; car parking in street
Meals breakfast, lunch, dinner
Prices rooms ⓔ-ⓔⓔ, breakfast ⓔ, meals ⓔ
Rooms 8 double, all with bath; all rooms have central heating, TV
Facilities bar/restaurant
Credit cards AE, MC, V
Children accepted **Disabled** access difficult **Pets** not accepted **Closed** never
Proprietor Carlos Morquilles

CARMONA

Venta de Carmona

~ Village hotel ~

Barrio del Palacio, 39554 Carmona, Cantabria
Tel & Fax (942) 728057

THERE are few villages as unspoilt and picturesque as Carmona with its unpaved streets and stone Cantabrian houses sheltering under variegated pantiled roofs.

The largest house in the village has been turned into a hotel by the regional government. The rooms are extremely varied. All have views either over the rooftops of the village or onto the great green slopes around. Several of them are reached across the large first floor lounge. Service is impersonal and consequently atmosphere is lacking inside the hotel but for that you only have to step outside.

~

Nearby village; Hermida gorge (35km); Saja beechwoods (25km).
Location at the top of the village
Meals breakfast, lunch, dinner
Prices rooms ⓔⓔ; breakfast ⓔ; meals ⓔⓔ
Rooms 6 double, 2 triple, all with bath; all rooms have central heating and phone
Facilities sitting-room, dining- room, bar
Credit cards V
Children accepted
Disabled access difficult
Pets not accepted **Closed** mid-Jan to early Mar **Manager** Teresa Martínez

CANTABRIA

QUIJAS, TORRELAVEGA

HOSTERIA DE QUIJAS
~ COUNTRY HOUSE HOTEL ~

Barrio Vinuesa s/n, 39590, Quijas, Reocín, Cantabria
TEL (942) 820833 FAX (942) 838050

After several years living abroad, the Castañeda family returned home to transform this palatial 18thC house near Torrelavega into an exemplary rural hotel.

The house, with its stone walls, spreading eaves, bay windows and timbered ceilings, has been restored with great care, especially noticeable in the former library (now the reception area) and the private oratory of a former owner (approved by a bull of Pope Leon XIII).

The hotel's most outstanding feature is the 4,000 square metre garden which surrounds it on three sides with hydrangeas, climbers, and a magnolia several hundred years old, under which you can sit. The terrace is covered by a shady grapevine.

Demetrio Castañeda and his daughter Sonia serve their guests in person. The restaurant enjoys a reputation of its own: Javier Sobrón, a local chef who once cooked for the King of Spain, supervises the excellent cooking which includes too many specialities, all exquisitely presented, to list in full.

It is a shame that the main Oviedo to Santander road, with its heavy traffic, runs so close to the hotel. When booking, make sure you ask for a room on the other side.

~

Nearby Santillana del Mar (4 km); Altamira caves (5 km).
Location on the main road from Oviedo to Santander; car parking and garden
Meals breakfast, lunch, dinner
Prices rooms €€-€€€€; breakfast €; meals €€€
Rooms 12 double, one single, 6 suites, all with bath; all rooms have central heating, telephone, TV (satellite), hairdrier, minibar
Facilities sitting-room, 2 dining-rooms, bar, terrace; garden, swimming-pool
Credit cards AE, DC, MC, V
Children welcome **Disabled** access difficult **Pets** not accepted
Closed 23 Dec to 4 Jan **Proprietor** Demetrio Castañeda

VIZCAYA

MUNDAKA

ATALAYA

TOWN HOTEL

Paseo de Txorrokopunta, 2, 48360, Mundaka, Vizcaya
TEL (94) 6177000 **FAX** (94) 6876899

There are no major changes to report at this turn-of-the-century house, with its bright white façade dominated by bay windows, which stands close to the fishing port of Mundaka at the mouth of the Ría de Guernica. It has been decorated in an English style and transformed into a small family hotel. Extremely well kept and run, it undoubtedly provides the best accommodation on this stretch of coast.

To enter, you have to use the intercom. You will be received by the owner, Mari Carmen Alonso, or her husband. Both exude Basque honesty and hospitality. An air-conditioned conservatory (without plants) serves as a breakfast room and bar, and for meals there is a new cafeteria and terrace. Bedrooms have been very carefully put together, with every detail attended to: the magazine racks, for instance, may well contain up-to-date foreign publications. They are, however, a little small, even if the beds themselves are large.

Through the bay windows there are views of the church, the adjacent beach and the Bay of Biscay where it meets the estuary. This is a place for anyone who appreciates silence and a seemingly home-like atmosphere.

Nearby Santa María church; Guernica, Basque capital (14 km).
Location in front of the port, on the Ría de Guernica; garden and car parking
Meals breakfast
Prices €€-€€€€; breakfast P
Rooms 10 double, 1 single, one suite, all with bath; all rooms have central heating, telephone, radio, TV (satellite), minibar
Facilities dining-room, sitting-room, bar, garden
Credit cards AE, DC, MC, V
Children welcome; baby-sitting service
Disabled obliging staff to help
Pets accepted **Closed** never
Proprietor Mari Carmen Alonso

GUIPUZCOA

HONDARRIBIA (FUENTERRABIA)

PAMPINOT
～ HISTORIC PALACE ～

Mayor, 3, 20280 Hondarribia (Fuenterrabía), Guipúzcoa
TEL (943) 640600 **FAX** (943) 645128

Olga Alvarez bought this palatial house in the oldest part of historic Hondarribia with the intention of living in it herself. Only after renovating it did she have the idea to convert it into a small and uniquely personal hotel with eight cosy rooms.

The building has almost as long a history as the town, whose steep streets and ramparts are a reminder of its former importance. Before becoming a hotel, the house served variously as a warehouse, cider brewery and aristocratic residence. With such a distinguished pedigree, it is, as you would expect, filled with antique furniture, chandeliers, plastered lintels, carpeted floors and other fine ornaments.

The bedrooms are spacious, comfortable and softly lit. The TV seems out of place, however, and the bathrooms are rather sparingly decorated. But the core of this place's appeal lies in the feminine touch, the sensitivity, and the good manners of Olga Alvarez and her team. Caution: streetside rooms can suffer from noise, and with no air-conditioning to allow windows to be closed, or ceiling fan, this has given a sleepless night to at least one visitor of whom we know. Reports welcome.
～

Nearby Castle of Carlos V, now a Parador; Jaizkíbel golf course (5 km); San Sebastian (21 km).
Location in the main street, in the historic city centre; no car parking
Meals breakfast
Prices rooms ⓔⓔⓔ-ⓔⓔⓔⓔ; breakfast ⓔ
Rooms 3 double, one single, 3 family rooms, one suite, all with bath; all rooms have central heating, telephone, TV, minibar, safe
Facilities sitting-room, bar, breakfast room
Credit cards AE, DC, MC, V
Children very welcome; games and stories available **Disabled** access difficult
Pets accepted **Closed** Nov
Proprietor Olga Alvarez

GUIPUZCOA

HONDARRIBIA (FUENTERRABIA)

PARADOR DE HONDARRIBIA
～ TOWN HOTEL ～

Plaza de Armas 14, 20280 Hondarribia, Guipuzcoa
TEL (943) 645 500 **FAX** (943)) 642 153

A 12thC fortress with walls ten feet (3 m) thick, originally built to protect Spain from French incursions, this is the oldest of northern Spain's paradors. (It is also known as PT el Emperador.) On a recent visit we immediately noticed the friendliness of the welcome and a feeling of warmth and elegance: quite a contrast to its bygone military grimness. Guests clearly find it easy to respond to this appeal.

In fact, our inspector described it as 'simply stunning'. There are some beautifully furnished public rooms, a bar, a cafe and 'the most wonderful inner courtyard'. There are impressive antiques throughout, and the conversion from castle to hotel has been done in 'the most pleasing way'. Bedrooms are attractive and individual.

The lack of a restaurant is no drawback: there's an excellent local selection. Our inspector recommends Sebastian, a short walk from the parador, with innovative Basque/French dishes.

～

Nearby Jaizkibel golf course; San Sebastian
Location centre of old city, close to church, singposted; own car parking
Meals breakfast
Price €€
Rooms 36, all with bath, heating
Facilities two drawing-rooms, cafe, breakfast room
Credit cards AE, DC, MC, V
Children welcome
Disabled no special facilities
Pets small ones accepted
Closed never
Manager Pilar Demiguel

ALAVA

PARADOR DE ARGOMANIZ
~ PALACE PARADOR ~

Ctra. N1, km 363 01192 Argomániz, Alava
TEL (945) 293200 FAX (945) 293287

The Parador is reached by a narrow lane branching off from the Madrid-Irun road near Vitoria. It stands on the slopes of Mount Zabalgaña, above the few humble houses of the village, from where it commands views of the sierras of Urbasa and Gorbea, Estíbaliz monastery, the Alava plains and Vitoria. It is a stone palace, built in the 17th century by the Larrea family: austere and monumental, it reflects the origins of its owners, knights of the Order of Calatrava and ministers of Spanish monarchs.

The reception hall and dining-room (formerly a granary) have handsome timbered ceilings. The decorative style is sober and distinctly Castilian – oil paintings, wall lamps, iron bolts – relieved by the antique furniture and potted plants typical of Paradors. 'Old-fashioned and in need of refurbishment' comments our inspector, who also thought it 'perfectly adequate' for an overnight stop – but not for a long stay.

The rooms have bay windows, a typical local feature, which make an attractive space in which to breakfast, while looking out over the green countryside. The bedroom floors and the bathrooms are arguably in need of attention. Perhaps the most memorable feature of this Parador is its silence: a place for early nights and sound sleep.

~

Nearby Vitoria (15 km); Estíbaliz Sanctuary (4 km); Zadorra reservoir (15 km).
Location in a small country village; garden and car parking
Meals breakfast, lunch, dinner
Prices rooms €€-€€€€; breakfast €; meals €€
Rooms 53 double, all with bath; all rooms have central heating, telephone, minibar, TV
Facilities 3 sitting-rooms, cafeteria, dining-room
Credit cards AE, DC, MC, V
Children welcome **Disabled** access easy **Pets** not accepted
Closed never
Manager Jorge Ridriguez

ALAVA

LAGUARDIA

CASTILLO EL COLLARDO
~ TOWN HOTEL ~

Paseo El Collado, 01300 Laguardia, Alava
TEL (941) 121 200 **FAX** (941) 600878

By repute, this is one of northern Spain's most interesting new hotels of the 1990s, but before putting it in the guide we decided to take a close look.

Castillo means a fortified manor house, but the building, with its distinctive tower, was originally a cosmetics factory. Later, under church ownership, it became a residence for priests. In 1981, Sr Javier, the current proprietor, fulfilled a long-standing ambition by buying it to convert into a hotel. It took ten years, and the result really is different from anywhere else you may have stayed: 'somewhat eccentric, but utterly charming.' It is furnished in a highly individual style, with beautiful woodwork and many art nouveau features, particularly tiles and glass. The eight bedrooms are all different, with contrasting colour schemes, ornate turn-of-the 20th century embossed radiators and oval baths. They offer luxury with an appealing hint of decadence.

There is a small bar and an enormous wine cellar, as befits the hotel's location in the heart of Rioja wine country. The restaurant 'has a personality of its own' and an extensive wine list. Climb the tower for views over vineyards and mountains. If you feel jaded by standardised hotels, this will freshen you up.

~

Nearby Vitoria (Gasteiz), Logrono, Soria
Location signposted in town. No private car parking; public parking nearby
Meals breakfast, lunch, dinner
Price €€
Rooms 8, all with bath, air-conditioning
Facilities sitting-room, dining-room, garden
Credit cards AE, DC, MC, V
Children welcome **Disabled** not especially suitable
Pets accepted by prior arrangement **Closed** never
Proprietors Sgr Javier

BASQUE COUNTRY/NAVARRA

HOTELS IN SAN SEBASTIAN AND PAMPLONA

VISITORS FROM BRITAIN tend to overlook the Basque country just over the French border in their hurry to explore the Picos or the coastline of Galicia to the west. Yet it has a lot to offer. Not least of the attractions is the smart seaside resort of San Sebastián (or Donostia – duplicate names are a constant reminder here of the Basque separatist movement). In a region noted for fine food, this is probably the gastronomic headquarters; sadly, none of the best restaurants has rooms. Two places to stay stand out, neither of them cheap: the big and charmless Monte Igueldo, which enjoys a heart-stopping view (especially at night) from the peak of the same name at one side of the sweeping Bahía de la Concha (Tel (943) 210211); and the lovely old seafront Hotel de Londres y de Inglaterra (Tel (943) 426989), as gracious a seaside hotel as you could wish for.

Thanks largely to Hemingway's novels, Pamplona is world-famous for its July fiesta. The bulls run under the windows of the centrally-located and old-fashioned La Perla (Tel (948) 227706. Upper rooms in the more peaceful, 28-room Eslava (Tel (948) 222270) look out on the countryside beyond the city walls.

PARADORES IN NORTH CENTRAL SPAIN

Those who arrive in Spain on the Santander ferry are in reach of three Paradores. The PT Gil Blas at Santillana del Mar (see page 45) is one of the best of the chain. The others are modern, but enjoy enviable positions in the mountains of the Picos de Europa. The otherwise dreary PT Río Deva at Fuente Dé is spectacularly set high up in a natural amphitheatre, close to a cable-car giving access to wonderful views and walks (Tel (942) 736651). PT Fuentes Carrionas is further south at Cervera de Pisuerga in the less spectacular foothills of the Picos, but is a rather more stylish hotel (Tel (979) 870075).

East and south-east of Santander are some wonderfully historic Paradores. The PT de Argómaniz, east of Vitoria, has 54 rooms in wings built on to a mellow 300-year-old mansion (see page 52). South of Pamplona is the PT Príncipe de Viana at Olite (medieval capital of Navarra), a fairy-tale castle of turrets and towers, with some splendid rooms within (Tel (948) 740000). The PT Marco Fabio Quintiliano at nearby Calahorra in La Rioja is a modern building of five floors with 62 rooms (Tel (941) 130358).

NAVARRA

YESA

Hospedería de Leyre

~ Monastery hotel ~

Monasterio de Leyre, 31410, Yesa, Navarra
Tel (948) 884100 **Fax** (948) 884137

Situated in a landscape of exceptional beauty, this hotel is housed is one of the outbuildings of the Benedictine monastery of Leyre, which was the political and spiritual centre of the kingdom of Navarra during the 11thC. From some of the rooms there is an unbeatable view of the valley; others overlook the old cloister, now a garden. The hotel is simple, even functional, but it is an ideal place to rest, to meditate or to use as a base from which to walk in the surrounding countryside. The restaurant serves typical Navarra food. If you want to sample monastic life, there are rooms (for men only) inside the monastery itself. A Dutch reader notes: 'Not a joyful place. Bar closed after dinner. Many visitors to the monastery at peak times.'

~

Nearby Foz de Lumbier gorge (4 km), Javier castle (8 km).
Location on the road from Yesa reservoir; car parking
Meals breakfast, lunch, dinner
Prices rooms €€; breakfast €, meals €€
Rooms 13 double, 14 single, 5 suites, all with bath; all rooms have central heating, phone **Facilities** dining-room, bar, meeting room, TV room
Credit cards AE, DC, V **Children** welcome **Disabled** no special facilities
Pets not accepted **Closed** mid-Dec to Mar **Manager** Mercedes Casado

PUENTE LA REINA

Méson del Peregrino

~ Restaurant-with-rooms ~

Ctra Pamplona Logroño, km 23, Puente la Reina, Navarra
Tel (948) 340075 **Fax** (948) 341190

This imitation-old timber and stone building sits beside a busy main road on the ancient pilgrim route to Santiago de Compostela. It has recently been taken over by distinguished restaurateurs and the rooms – formerly small and dark, have been attractively redecorated.

The split level restaurant with its subdued lighting, sloping beamed ceilings and stone arches is a delight. Potted plants and collections of curios contrast with the bare stone floors and walls. Even without the improvements planned for the bedrooms this is a comfortable place for an overnight stop and a great meal.

~

Nearby Pilgrim's bridge 1.5km; Estella (19km); Olite (28km).
Location 1km from the town centre on the road from Pamplona; garden and car parking
Meals breakfast, lunch, dinner
Prices rooms €€-€€€€; breakfast € meals €€€
Rooms 14 double, all with bath; all rooms have telephone, TV
Facilities dining-room, bar; swimming-pool
Credit cards MC, V **Children** welcome; play area **Disabled** no special facilities
Pets accepted **Closed** restaurant only 24 Dec to 3 Jan
Proprietor Angelo Camberro and Angelines Sedano

LA RIOJA

HARO

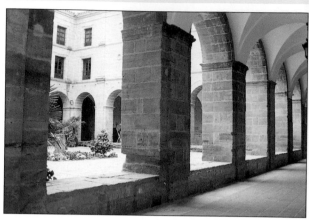

LOS AGUSTINOS

～ CONVERTED MONASTERY ～

San Agustin, 2, 26200, Haro, La Rioja
TEL (941) 311308 **FAX** (941) 303148

In times past the famous wine growing areas of La Rioja had many monasteries and convents lodging pilgrims on the road to Santiago de Compostela. This deconsecrated Augustinian monastery in the centre of Haro still houses latter-day travellers but in more luxury than their pious predecessors.

The building, with its massively thick walls, has also been used as an arsenal, hospital, school and town prison: you can still read the graffitti, with names and dates, written by prisoners on the columns of the magnificent cloister.

Another highlight of the hotel is the sitting-room, a vast chamber crossed by great arches, containing various tapestries and a grand piano. The dining-room, bar and other public rooms, though, are non-descript. For a special room book number 124 in which the bed lies in a recess with a stone arch overhead. Otherwise the rooms are disappointingly characterless. Six of them on the second floor have views over the patio.

This is a useful centre for visiting the surrounding bodegas (wineries) which have made La Rioja famous. A major event in June is Haro's annual 'Battle of Wine'.

～

Nearby St Thomas's church; bodegas, vineyards and entomological centre; Bilibio crags.
Location in the town centre; no car parking
Meals breakfast, lunch, dinner
Prices rooms €€€-€€€€; breakfast €; meals €€
Rooms 54 double, 6 single, 2 suites all with bath; all rooms have air-conditioning, telephone, TV (satellite) minibar, hairdrier
Facilities 4 conference rooms, sitting-room, bar, dining- room; interior cloisters
Credit cards AE, DC, V
Children welcome **Disabled** access easy; lift/elevator **Pets** accepted **Closed** never
Proprietors Jesús de Miguel

BURGOS

BURGOS

HOTEL LANDA PALACE

~ ROADSIDE HOTEL ~

Carretera Madrid km 235, 09000, Burgos
TEL (947) 257777 **FAX**(947) 264676

Forget real palaces for a moment; this is the eccentric dream of one Señora Landa. Some consider it luxurious, charmingly over-the-top or supremely pretentious; we see it as great fun. A sense of excess is aroused by the prodigious collection of old horse carts outside; but inside you are positively whisked away from reality into a Gothic fantasy. The tower you step into, transported to this convenient roadside location from a neighbouring village, is the only genuinely old part of the hotel. All the rest – including the Gothic vaults over the larger dining-room and the swimming-pool, and the carved spiral staircases – was built in the 60s.

The bedrooms are no less excessive. The grand suite has doors of polished walnut and a brass bedstead surmounted by a crown. Its sitting-room – containing a massive antique desk and five-seater settee – could house a numerous family. But don't look out of the romantic, *ajimez* window or the spell will be broken by the sight of the main Burgos-Madrid road.

There are antiques and greenery everywhere, and surprises at every turn. The corridor outside the dining-rooms ticks to the rhythm of umpteen wall clocks.

~

Nearby Burgos; Miraflores Carthusian Monastery (5 km).
Location on main road to Madrid; with garden and car parking
Meals breakfast, lunch, dinner
Prices rooms €€€€; breakfast €€; dinner €€€
Rooms 34 double, 3, single, 5 suites, all with bath; all rooms have central heating, air-conditioning, phone, TV; most rooms have hairdrier
Facilities dining-room, 4 sitting-rooms, bar, swimming-pool
Credit cards not accepted
Children welcome; baby-sitting available **Disabled** access difficult; lift
Pets not accepted **Closed** never
Manager Francisco Javier Revuelta

BURGOS

BURGOS

MESON DEL CID
～ CITY HOTEL ～

Plaza Santa Maria 8, 09003, Burgos
TEL (947) 208715 **FAX** (947) 269460

Opposite the Cathedral and on its own little square, this hotel looks like a pleasingly proportioned, much overgrown cottage. Its owner is a book-collector – most appropriate, as Burgos is a city associated with early printing – and almost the first thing that you will see inside is a reproduction of an illuminated manuscript on display in the hall. Not, as it turns out, the famous El Cid poem, which is the theme of the rest of the hotel.

Although it is not an old building, it has been decorated with great style and sensitivity. The floors and bedrooms are named after kings, queens and other characters from El Cid. Particularly striking are the bathrooms, with out-of-the-ordinary matt porcelain basins and chunky brass taps. The bedroom furniture is antique or reproduction, with iron and brass bedsteads and some fine details such as a black-and-brass phone in one room.

Best of the public rooms is the basement bar with black chairs and marble-topped tables. The next-door disco doubles inadequately as a sitting-room. The dining-room upstairs is rectangular and low-ceilinged; there is also a separate public restaurant, connected to the hotel by a passageway, with a choice of rooms.

～

Nearby Cathedral; Miraflores Carthusian Monastery (4 km).
Location in front of cathedral in city centre; with private garage
Meals breakfast, lunch, dinner
Prices rooms €€€-€€€€; breakfast €; dinner €€
Rooms 21 double, 5 single, 3 suites, all with bath; all rooms have central heating, phone, TV, radio
Facilities dining-room, sitting-room/disco, bar
Credit cards AE, DC, MC, V
Children welcome; baby-sitting available
Disabled access easy; lift/elevator **Pets** accepted
Closed never
Proprietor José López

BURGOS

COVARRUBIAS

HOTEL ARLANZA
~ VILLAGE HOTEL ~

Plaza de Doña Urraca, 09346, Covarrubias, Burgos
TEL (947) 406441 **FAX** (947) 406359
E-MAIL arlanza@ctv.es

The Arlanza takes up one side of an attractive cobbled square (closed to traffic) in a clean, prettily restored village full of half-timbered houses, shady porticoes and flowery balconies.

It is not one of those hotels brimming over with space and facilities, and is all the more refreshing for this. But, with black beams overhead and a handsome, wide, tiled staircase, it has some character. The sitting-room ('smokey', notes a recent visitor), is combined with the bar, and there Is nowhere else pleasant to sit. You'll eat adequately in the dining-room, which is dimly lit by one small window. The Castilian soup is served so hot that it has to be eaten with a wooden spoon. Wild boar – plentiful in these parts, and a nocturnal traffic hazard until the start of the hunting season – is served in rich savoury slices.

The bedrooms, leading off dark corridors paved with squeaky red tiles, are very simply furnished. There is an occasional clash of striped and stippled marbles and the bathrooms are in need of improvement. But you get no more or less than you need for a comfortable night.

~

Nearby Santo Domingo de Silos and Yecla Gorge (20 km), Quintanilla de las Viñas (25 km).
Location on main square; no car parking in square
Meals breakfast, lunch, dinner
Prices rooms €€€; breakfast €; dinner €€
Rooms 32 double, 2 single, 2 suites, one family room, all with bath; all rooms have central heating, phone
Facilities 2 dining-rooms, sitting-room, bar
Credit cards AE, DC, V
Children welcome
Disabled access easy, lift/elevator
Pets accepted **Closed** 12 Dec to 1 Mar
Proprietor Juan José Ortiz

Burgos

SANTO DOMINGO DE SILOS

HOTEL TRES CORONAS DE SILOS

∼ VILLAGE HOTEL ∼

Plaza Mayor 6, 09610, Santo Domingo de Silos, Burgos
TEL (947) 390047 **FAX** (947) 390065

aA charming, peaceful establishment, so unpretentious that it doubles as the village newsagents, this is the place to come if you want to be undisturbed. You can hear the birds singing – though in high season you must wait until the coach parties go home.

The hotel is the dominant house on the village square, with a semi-circular arched doorway and a proud coat of arms over its central balcony (which belongs to room number 9, by the way). Inside, there is an overwhelming effect of renovated stone and ancient, seasoned wood (all of it skilful reproduction). Each of the rooms has at least one bare stone wall, an ample ration of solid furniture and a large, tinted mirror. Those at the front of the building look out on to the square through leaded lights fringed with stained glass.

The bar is small, frequently dominated by the TV and insufficently lit to write in, and the only sitting-area is on the second floor landing. The dining-room includes its own wood-fired roasting oven. (But for half the price of a menu here you can get a good, although more casual, meal in the Hostal Santo Domingo de Silos, a minute's walk away, prepared and served by a delightfully jolly landlady.)

∼

Nearby Monastery and cloister; Yecla Gorge (5 km).
Location near monastery, in main square; car parking on square
Meals breakfast, lunch, dinner
Prices rooms €-€€; breakfast €; lunch €€-€€€, dinner €€
Rooms 14 double, 2 single, all with bath; all rooms have central heating, phone
Facilities dining-room, bar
Credit cards AE, MC, V
Children welcome
Disabled access impossible **Pets** not accepted
Closed never
Proprietor Emeterio Martín

ZARAGOZA

NUÉVALOS

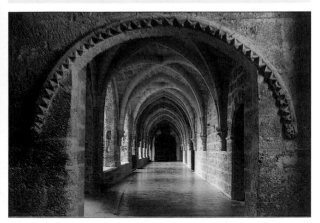

MONASTERIO DE PIEDRA

~ FORMER MONASTERY ~

50210, Nuévalos, Zaragoza
TEL (976) 849011 **FAX** (976) 849054

It is not often that you will find alabaster window panes in a hotel, but glass was not available to the seven Cistercian monks and their abbot who, in the 12th century, founded what is today one of Spain's most intriguing hotels.

The echoing, cavernous corridors – hung with signs imploring silence, and chilly in winter – might as well be time tunnels leading you back to the first millennium AD. If you know where to look, you can still see traces of the castle on top of which the monks built – machicolations and parts of the moat – breaking through centuries of masonry. Beside the cloisters there is a dank Romanesque passageway that may date from as early as the 7th century. The enormous staircase, with vaulting and fading frescoes above will leave you with a stiff neck.

The bedrooms are varied and were renovated (together with the bathrooms) recently enough. The best of them is Room 206, on its own entresol up a private staircase. Many look out on to the beautiful park, full of rocks and waterfalls (visible from the hotel when the leaves fall in autumn), that attracts vast numbers of visitors annually; hotel guests receive a complimentary ticket for both this and the Cloisters.

The hotel is busy with adult education courses in summer.

~

Nearby Maluenda (40 km); scenic road to Turmiel (45 km).
Location at entrance to park of same name, a few kilometres outside Nuévalos; with garden and car park
Meals breakfast, lunch, dinner
Prices rooms €€-€€€€; breakfast € dinner €€
Rooms 44 double, 8 single, 9 family rooms, all with bath; all rooms have central heating, phone, TV, safe
Facilities sitting-room, bar, TV rooms, games room, dining-room, swimming-pool, tennis court, terrace **Credit cards** AE, DC, MC, V **Children** welcome
Disabled ramp access and specially adapted facilities
Pets accepted only in rooms **Closed** never **Manager** José María Montaner

HUESCA/LÉRIDA

HOTELS IN HUESCA AND LÉRIDA

THE PROVINCES OF HUESCA AND LÉRIDA are not on the track beaten by most foreign tourists. This is not to say that they have nothing to offer the visitor, but the major attractions are the outdoor activities and scenery of the Pyrenees, the mountains forming the border with France, and rightly or wrongly these are not the usual target of non-Spanish holiday-makers. Not surprisingly, the best hotels are concentrated here; access is not easy – even by Alpine standards, the Pyrenean roads can be tortuous and slow.

The feature box on page 70 includes several mountain hotels, including the PT del Monte Perdido, just to the east of the spectacular Monte Perdido massif, which forms part of a very impressive National Park. On the other side of the Park there is simple but satisfactory accommodation to be found in and around Torla; the 70-room Ordesa is beautifully situated (Tel (974) 486125). The Paradores at Viella and Arties are mainly ski-oriented; an interesting alternative to the latter for gastronomes (but closed in early summer and early winter) is the Michelin- starred 30-room Valartiés (Tel (973) 640801). Lérida does not attract many visitors and is not notably well prepared to receive them, but Huesca is a pleasant place with some interesting sights. Best-in-town (it does not face much opposition) is the smooth 120-room Pedro I de Aragón, just outside the centre (Tel (974) 220300).

Faus-Hutte

⁓ Mountain hotel ⁓

Ctra. de Francia, km 658.5 22870, Villanúa, Huesca
Tel (974) 378136 **Fax** (974) 378198

At the foot of the 2,886-metre Mount Collarada, on the right bank of the River Aragón, sits the little town of Villanúa. Some years ago, Agustín Faus realized that this was an ideal setting for a cosy hotel offering a peaceful refuge in both winter and summer. The result is a hotel in Alpine style making much use of wood: parquet floors, panelled walls, heavy shutters and balconies on which to sit in a rocking chair and gaze at the view. Sr. Faus has seen to it that you will be warm at night beneath a feather quilt. 'Our customers are friends and they feel more at home than at home', he promises in his brochure.

⁓

Nearby Aruej Romanesque chapel; Las Guixas cave.
Location on the main road towards the Collarada; garden, car parking and garage
Meals breakfast, lunch, dinner
Prices rooms €€-€€€€€; breakfast €; meals €€
Rooms 7 double, one single, one suite, one family room, all with bath; all rooms have central heating, telephone, TV
Facilities dining-room, bar; terrace; gymnasium,2 sitting-rooms; guided trekking excursions **Credit cards** AE, DC, V **Children** welcome **Disabled** access easy
Pets accepted **Closed** never
Proprietor Agustín Faus

HUESCA

FORMIGAL

VILLA DE SALLENT
~ MOUNTAIN HOTEL ~

Urbanización Formigal, 22640, Sallent de Gállego, Huesca
TEL (974) 490223 **FAX** (974) 490150

Fidel Tejero and his family, owners of a well-known restaurant, invested all their savings in this stone and slate hotel situated at the foot of the ski slopes of Formigal, the ski resort in the Tena Valley of the Pyrenees. As you enter the hall you almost feel that you are in Switzerland or Scandinavia, rather than Spain. The wood panelling, pine furniture, the indirect lighting and the linen curtains are restful and charming.

The rooms are perfectly sealed to resist the cold. Watching the snow fall past your window while you are under a hot shower is not the least of the pleasures of this place. The bathrooms are small, however, and the bedroom walls thin.

Villa de Sallent is as comfortable for a snowed-in winter week, spent by the fireplace in the sitting-room, as for a month in summer, spent walking – walking is good not only from here but from other centres in the valley, particularly Sallent, off the C136.

There is a convenient lift to take you directly from the garage-cum-ski store to your bedroom at the end of an exhausting day's skiing. As you ascend, there is also the happy thought that Fidel is in the kitchen preparing supper.

~

Nearby France (6 km); Panticosa spa (21 km); Jaca (49 km).
Location on the hill of the estate, near the church and the ski office; garage with ski store
Meals breakfast, lunch, dinner
Prices rooms €€€; breakfast €; meals €€
Rooms 36 double, 4 single, one suite, all with bath; all rooms have central heating, telephone, TV
Facilities sitting-room, bar, dining-room
Credit cards AE, DC, MC, V
Children welcome; 20% discount
Disabled lift/elevator, obliging staff
Pets not accepted **Closed** never **Proprietor** Fidel Tejero

LÉRIDA

LA SEU D'URGELL

EL CASTELL

~ MOUNTAIN HOTEL ~

Ctra. de Lérida a Puigcerdà, km 129, 25700, La Seu d'Urgell, Lérida
TEL (973) 350704 **FAX** (973) 351574

This hotel is 10 kilometres from the border with Andorra, in the Urgellet Valley. A low-lying modern building of wood and slate, it sits snugly and unobtrusively under the castle of Seu d'Urgell. Its long line of balconies gives impressive views of the Cadí mountains.

The interior is intimate and sumptuous, but not affected. Owners Jaume Tàpies and his wife Ludi have managed to create one of the most welcoming atmospheres in the Catalan Pyrenees. They pay more than due attention to the kitchen, of which they feel especially proud and which has had some outstanding reviews. The menu includes Catalan mountain dishes (wild boar and pigs' trotters) but is also influenced by the proximity of France, evident in the exquisite foie gras and the interesting wine list. The dining-room has large windows opening on to the River Segre and the town of La Seu, which has a magnificent Romanesque cathedral.

A distinguished clientèle, more used to grand city hotels, comes here at weekends and holidays for the peace of the mountains and the rich living. It's an excellent base for skiing or hiking in the mountains, or for shopping in Andorra. Enthusiastic reports keep coming in. Only problem: the need to book well ahead.

~

Nearby castle; La Seu d'Urgell cathedral; Andorra (10 km); Sant Joan de l'Erm ski resort (30 km).
Location on top of a hill with views of the valley of Urgellet; car parking and garden
Meals breakfast, lunch, dinner
Prices rooms €€€-€€€€; breakfast €; meals €€€
Rooms 34 double, 4 suites,
all with bath; all rooms have air-conditioning, telephone, minibar, radio, TV (satellite), safe **Facilities** dining-room, cafeteria, meeting room, terrace; swimming-pool **Credit cards** AE, DC, MC, V **Children** welcome
Disabled no special facilities **Pets** accepted
Closed restaurant only, Jan 7 to Feb 7 **Proprietor** Jaume Tàpies i Travé

LÉRIDA

TREMP

CASA GUILLA
∼ VILLAGE GUEST HOUSE ∼

Santa Engràcia, Tremp 25636, Lérida
TEL & FAX (973) 252080 **E-MAIL** casaguilla@ctv.es
WEBSITE www.ctv.es/USERS/casaguilla

Britons Richard and Sandra Loder opened this ancient, labyrinthine stone farmhouse on the edge of a rock as a guest-house in 1986.

The former granaries and animal pens have become bedrooms, part of the stables a bar, the hayloft a sitting-room-cum-library and the farmyard a terrace overlooking the two lakes of the Tremp valley from a height of 1000m.

This is still the Loders' home and although the house will take 10-15 people they prefer to keep the numbers down 'so that our guests can feel the house is theirs to come and go freely from.' On the edge of a nature reserve, Casa Guilla is popular with naturalists.

Guests pay for half-board with discounts for meals not taken. Everyone eats together around the same table shipboard style. 'When you have the right mix of people,' says Sandra Loder, 'everything goes fine.' If after-dinner conversation is not for you there are a TV, video and board games in the sitting-room.

The village of Santa Engràcia can be hard to find and you'd be wise to ask the Loders to send you directions in advance.

∼

Nearby hang gliding centre (43 km); Aigues Torres National Park (80km); ski resorts (110 km); Andorra (110 km).
Location from Tremp take C147 towards Pobla de Segur. After 2 km turn left at sign to Santa Engràcia. Follow road 10 km to Santa Engràcia (house is near church); car parking
Meals breakfast, snack lunch, dinner
Prices bed, breakfast and evening meal €€; snack lunch €
Rooms 4 double, 1 family room
Facilities sitting-room, dining-room, bar, library; terrace, swimming-pool
Credit cards not accepted
Children accepted
Disabled Dec to Mar **Pets** accepted
Closed never **Proprietor** Richard Loder

Tarragona

Masía del Cadet

~ Country house hotel ~

Les Masies de Poblet, 43440, L'Espluga de Francolí, Tarragona
Tel (977) 870869 **Fax** (977) 870496

This 15thC masía or manor house, has been restored by the Corominas-Vidal family with great care and intelligence and opened in 1990 as a model Catalan country hotel. Their act is unbeatable in the region, and at prices much lower than many other hotels in its class.

The family offers a friendly welcome, and the restaurant serves traditional Catalan cuisine. However, we have had one very negative letter about it since our last edition – reports especially welcome.

An ideal base for a visit to Poblet's Cistercian monastery, a superb example of medieval architecture, which can claim to be a must for any visitor to this part of Spain.

~

Nearby Espluga museum; Poblet monastery (2 km)
Location near Poblet monastery; car parking
Meals breakfast, lunch, dinner
Prices rooms €€; breakfast €; lunch €€€, dinner €€
Rooms 12 double, all with bath; all rooms have central heating, telephone, radio, TV (optional)
Facilities dining-room, bar, TV room, sitting-room swimming-pool **Credit cards** AE, DC, MC, V **Children** welcome; play area in garden **Disabled** access easy; lift **Pets** not accepted **Closed** never **Proprietor** Mercè Vidal

---

PARADORES IN NORTH-EAST SPAIN

THE PYRENEES HAVE A HANDFUL OF remote modern Paradores. The most remote is the PT del Monte Perdido near Bielsa, hidden in a beautiful valley of bubbling mountain streams; the 24 rooms are appropriately rustic and the fireplace is the focal point (Tel (974) 501011). The PT Valle de Arán at Viella and the PT Don Gaspar de Portolá at Arties are separated only by 6 km of bumpy mountain road. Both come into their own in winter, serving the smart ski resort of Baqueira-Beret. The Viella Parador (135 rooms) has a semi-circular glass lounge to allow panoramic views (Tel (973)640100), and the Arties Parador (40 rooms) is stuffed with hunting trophies and easy chairs (Tel (973) 640801). Just south of Andorra is the PT Seo de Urgel; the modern hotel incorporates an ancient cloister, now filled with plants and functional sofas (Tel (973) 352000).

Further south are two impressive hilltop Paradores, at Cardona and Vich (see pages 74 and 80). And to the west, out of the mountains, the 66-room PT Fernando de Aragón in the captivating hilltop village of Sos del Rey Catolicó (the famous Fernando's birthplace) – one of the best modern Paradores (Tel (948) 888011). The modern 87-room PT de la Costa Brava at Aiguablava is chiefly remarkable for its splendid cliff-top setting (Tel (972) 622162). Further south and a little way inland is the PT Castillo de la Zuda at Tortosa (tel.(977) 444450).

TARRAGONA

ESPLUGA DE FRANCOLI

HOSTAL DEL SENGLAR
⬳ COUNTRY HOTEL ⬳

Pl Montserrat Canals, 143440, Espluga de Francoli, Tarragona
TEL (977) 870121 **FAX** (977) 870127
E-MAIL hostaldelsenglar@net-way.net **WEBSITE** www.hostalsenglar@worldonline.es

Built in 1965, this three-storey whitewashed and terracotta-roofed hostal is now almost completely obscured by the evergreen trees of its own garden, together with those of the neighbouring civic park.

It is a white-walled and wooden-beamed labyrinth inside. The many-chambered dining-hall, with its wooden balconies, nooks, crannies and murals of country scenes, is highly festive when full, and pleasantly intimate when not. The five-course Menu de Calcotada is an appropriately medieval feast – a traditional celebration of the vine and onion crops specific to the area (calcots is Catalan for shallots).

There is yet more timber and pottery in the salon, together with well-upholstered reproduction furniture from which the garden can comfortably be viewed. On Saturday evenings in August there is a splendid barbecue under the trees.

The bright bedrooms have stout wood and leather chairs, and decent-sized tables in addition to good, solid beds. Generous rugs add warmth to the red-tiled floors, and plants, pots and original oil-paintings are dotted around.

⬳

Nearby Poblet Monastery, (2 km); Museum of Rural Life in L'Espluga.
Location up hill from main square in civic gardens; with garden and car parking
Meals breakfast, lunch, dinner
Prices rooms €-€€€; breakfast €; lunch €€€, dinner €€€
Rooms 30 double, 10 single, 2 suites, all with bath; all rooms have central heating, phone, radio; some have TV
Facilities dining-room, sitting-room, TV room, disco; swimming-pool, tennis court
Credit cards AE, DC, MC, V
Children welcome; special menus; play area in garden
Disabled access easy; lift/elevator; ground-floor rooms
Pets not accepted
Closed never **Manager** Pedro Fernandez

Barcelona

Hotels in Barcelona

Most of the hotels in the lively and captivating city of Barcelona (which hosted the 1992 Olympic Games) are in the centre, in two areas – around the Plaça Catalunya and Las Ramblas (the broad, leafy avenue that leads to the sea), and around the cathedral and the medieval quarter (Barrio Gótico).

The Plaça de Catalunya has the more traditional grand hotels, such as the Ritz (Tel (93) 318 5200), an imposing building of 1919 with an abundance of gold-leaf and marble, and recently refurbished palatial rooms making it one of Barcelona's best. The Gran Vía (described on page 73) is another old charmer, as is the Avenida Palace (Tel (93) 301 9600), dignified and extremely popular, with excellent service and welcome. The Regente (Tel (93) 487 5989) has the added bonus of a roof-top swimmingpool. Further out, near the Francescá Macià Plaza, is a very British establishment, the Derby (Tel (93) 322 3215) which is smart and subdued, and, should you be in need, has Guinness on tap.

Of the Barrio Gótico hotels, the Colón (Tel (93) 301 1404) is an old favourite with tourists. It stands opposite the magnificent Gothic cathedral (ask for a front room with a balcony or a sixth-floor room with a terrace) and a stone's throw from many of the city's sights. Rooms have elegant high ceilings and comfortable furniture. The Suizo (described below) is not far from here.

Hotel Suizo

~ City hotel ~

Plaza del Angel 12, 08002, Barcelona
Tel (93) 310 6108 **Fax** (93) 315 0461

Just behind the cathedral, the Hotel Suizo could not be better placed. Inside it is really more Parisien than Swiss. Marble-topped tables, bentwood chairs and stools line the opulent wooden bar and fill the stylish cafeteria upstairs (where breakfast is served). The large restaurant is invariably busy; the four-course menu offers ample choice and changes daily. Attic bedrooms have the most character, with effective blinds on the skylights, and light parquet floors. Some of the other rooms have lino floors, but all are well furnished in dark oak. The staff can seem somewhat stretched, particularly at check-out time, but are helpful.

~

Nearby Cathedral, museums, Gothic quarter, Las Ramblas.
Location behind cathedral; car parking can be arranged
Meals breakfast, lunch, dinner
Prices rooms €€-€€€; breakfast €; meals €€
Rooms 44 double, 5 single, one suite, all with bath; all rooms have central heating, air-conditioning, phone, TV, minibar, radio, safe
Facilities dining-room, TV room, snack bar, sitting-room
Credit cards AE, DC, MC, V
Children welcome **Disabled** access easy; lift/elevator **Pets** accepted **Closed** never
Manager Miguel Gargallo

BARCELONA

BARCELONA

HOTEL GRAN VIA
~ CITY HOTEL ~

Gran Vía 642, 08007, Barcelona
TEL (93) 318 1900 **FAX** (93) 318 9997

In the hell of Barcelona's traffic, the Gran Vía could not be easier to find: entering the city from the airport, on the main street of the same name, you pass it on the right.

A large town house, it does not look much from the outside, but once through the double-doored entrance, it is very grand. An impressive staircase sweeps up to the mezzanine, with its palatial dining-room in burgundy and grey and co-ordinating regency chairs. Here, English-speaking guests can have fun explaining to the Spanish-speaking matron who serves the extensive international breakfast how they want their bacon and eggs.

Above is another fine room – a salon with stucco ceiling and many antiques – and, true to Spanish form, there is a huge television stuck in the middle of the room. Beyond is a gorgeous roof terrace.

The bedrooms, set around the gallery, have all been renovated and refurbished. The air-conditioning is effective, if a bit noisy, and the Gran Vía displays the kind of ageing grandeur that is hard to resist. The staff remember you and you remember them. An American reader tells us that the fairly recent change of management has been for the good.

~

Nearby Las Ramblas; cathedral, museums.
Location set back from Gran Vía, near Plaza Cataluña; with garden and car parking
Meals breakfast only
Prices rooms €€€-€€€€; breakfast €
Rooms 37 double, 11 single, all with bath; all rooms have central heating, air-conditioning, phone, minibar
Facilities breakfast-room, sitting/TV room, terrace
Credit cards AE, DC, MC, V
Children accepted
Disabled no special facilities; lift/elevator
Pets not accepted **Closed** never
Manager José Luis García

BARCELONA

PT DUQUES DE CARDONA

~ HILLTOP PARADO ~

Castillo s/n, 08261, Cardona, Barcelona
TEL (93) 869 1275 **FAX** (93) 869 1636

Perched high on a hill above the Cardener river, this impressive medieval castle, built round an ancient collegiate church with parts dating back to the beginning of the 9th century, commands magnificent views in all directions, including the mountainous slag heaps from the potassium chlorate mine in the valley below.

The church itself is a popular tourist attraction, with guided tours morning and afternoon. But for local Spaniards, and some not so local, the main attraction is the food: an innovative menu and seasonal carte of house specialities and rare local dishes – country soups, rich fish stews, and desserts – served in the atmospheric stone-arched halls of the Bodegon restaurant (appropriately named, English-speaking visitors may think). Barcelonians will think nothing of driving the 100 km just to eat here.

There is little concession to medieval ascetism in other respects, though in terms of style, furnishings are faithful to the period of the building. Bedrooms range from extravagant suites with two four-posters to more modest twins, but all are immaculately furnished and clean. The three-chambered sitting-room is all rugs and leather armchairs, and free of TV. Staff put the comfort of their guests first.

~

Nearby Cardona; Salt Museum; Manresa (32 km).
Location on hill top near Cardona, visible for miles; with garden and car parking
Meals breakfast, lunch, dinner
Prices rooms €€€€; breakfast €, dinner €€
Rooms 52 double, 7 single, one suite, all with bath; all rooms have central heating, air-conditioning, phone, TV, minibar, safe
Facilities 2 dining-rooms, sitting-room, cafeteria, patio, 5 conference rooms
Credit cards AE, DC, MC, V
Children welcome
Disabled access difficult **Pets** not accepted
Closed never **Manager** Pedro Sonia

BARCELONA

HOTEL SANT BERNAT
~ COUNTRY HOTEL ~

Finca El Cot 08460, Montseny, Barcelona
TEL & FAX (93) 847 3011

Hidden away up a tiny track off the winding Tona road, amid the dense low forest of the lush Montseny Sierra, this large, attractive terracotta-roofed villa, built in the 50s and now covered in vines, is a sleepy delight. The grounds are glorious, with a willow tree, pond and fountain to the front, and a stone terrace, and the charming little chapel of Sant Bernat behind. You can stand peacefully admiring the view, or listen to the water trickling down the mountainside.

Inside, it is equally serene, though at times the TV in reception is liable to intrude. A series of restful sitting-rooms with fireplaces, leather chairs and rugs lead past the bar to the comfortable dining-room, prettily decorated with floral upholstery, wooden panelled pillars and fresh flowers. The spotless bedrooms are equally attractive, and contain all the extras, from full-length mirrors down to a free comb.

Lunch and dinner involve a three-course fixed menu which changes every day, supplemented by a short but interesting *carte*. There are regular services in the chapel on Sundays and holidays, and recitals on the Feast of St Bernard in June. A regular thought that food and welcome might have been 'down' since his last visit.

~

Nearby Montseny (8 km); Montseny Sierra.
Location in mountains, up tiny road from Montseny to Tona; with garden and car parking
Meals breakfast, lunch, dinner
Prices rooms €€-€€€; breakfast €; dinner €€
Rooms 18 double, 2 family rooms, all with bath; all rooms have central heating, phone, TV, hairdrier, safe
Facilities dining-room, 2 sitting-rooms, bar
Credit cards AE, DC, V
Children accepted **Disabled** no special facilities **Pets** not accepted **Closed** never
Manager Juan Miguel Pérez

BARCELONA

VILANOVA I LA GELTRU

HOTEL CÉSAR

~ RESORT HOTEL ~

Isaac Peral 4-8, 08800 Vilanova i la Geltrú, Barcelona
TEL (93) 8151125 **FAX** (93) 815 6719
E-MAIL hcesar@vvirtual.es

A four-storey white building with mediterraean blue paintwork around the windows, the César has been built up by the same family over four generations and more than 100 years.

Although from the outside it seems like just another block-shaped resort hotel, inside this one has a touch of taste without pretension. Classical music plays downstairs and the bar houses a small library.

The rooms are decorated simply but with interest using a variety of carefully chosen modern fabrics. All of them look onto the patio below and from the higher floors you can see the sea. The choice is the Albéniz suite on the first floor in which a fine china tea service and packet of Earl Grey awaits you in a homely sitting-room with cane furniture and a pine desk.

Much of the hotel's trade is from business groups and the public rooms reflect this with two conference rooms squeezing the sitting-room into a minimal area in front of reception. In good weather, however, the patio will meet most needs.

The restaurant, La Fitorra, is adjacent to the hotel in an old fisherman's cottage with a pleasant patio of its own at the back.

~

Nearby Casa Papiol, castle and Balaguer Museum; Sitges (7km); Vilafranca del Penedès palace and wine museum (20km).
Location behind Ribes Roges beach; car parking on street
Meals breakfast, lunch, dinner
Prices rooms €€-€€€€; breakfast P, meals from €
Rooms 28 double, 2 suites, all with bath; all rooms have air-conditioning, central heating, TV, minibar, phone, safe
Facilities dining-room, bar, 2 conference rooms, sauna/ solarium, hydromassage pool **Credit cards** AE, DC, MC, V
Children accepted
Disabled lift **Pets** accepted
Closed restaurant only Sun dinner, Mon and Jan
Proprietor Esther Nolla

BARCELONA

HOTEL ROMÀNTIC
~ SEASIDE HOTEL ~

Sant Isidre 33, 08870, Sitges, Barcelona
TEL (93) 894 8375

Gonçal Sobrer i Barea is passionately in love with his careful restoration of three 19thC town villas, originally built by Catalan rum barons returning from Cuba. He has good cause. This is a real rarity, and, considering it merits, very modestly priced. With its airy halls, blue and white tiles, sculptures, marble bays and ceramics, it could easily be the setting for a novel by García Marquez – or perhaps Graham Greene. In the club-style bar (the bar itself being an original imported from Cuba) you half-expect to spot Our Man From Havana sipping a rum while ensconced in one of the creaking wicker chairs.

Even the old stone washing troughs are preserved (though no longer in use). All the bedrooms are individually furnished with genuine antiques from the period, with original paintings and ceramics. Señor Sobrer is proud that they contain not a single 'mod con' (save, of course, en suite bathrooms), and there are few comfortable sofas; but this is the nineteenth century, after all. Sadly, only breakfast is served in the palmed, patio-garden these days: a shame, since it would be a most 'romantic' setting for a longer, leisurely meal. We can only apologize for not mentioning in earlier editions that this is a gay hotel – though none the less charming for that. If you're 'hetero', it may not be for you.
~

Nearby Old Sitges, museums, main beach.
Location in side-street in heart of old city; with large garden, no car parking
Meals breakfast
Prices €€-€€€; breakfast €
Rooms 34 double, 30 with shower, 4 with bath; 18 single, 3 with wash-basin, 15 with shower; all rooms have phone, fans
Facilities 3 sitting-rooms, bar
Credit cards AE, V **Children** welcome **Disabled** no special facilities **Pets** accepted
Closed 1 Nov to 15 Mar
Proprietor Gonçal Sobrer i Barea

BARCELONA

LA SANTA MARIA
~ SEASIDE HOTEL ~

Passeig de la Ribera 52, 08870, Sitges, Barcelona
TEL (93) 894 0999 **FAX** (93) 894 7871

So successful is La Santa María in the centre of smart Sitges, that it expanded to having two restaurants – both on the seafront – and almost doubled the number of bedrooms. It is still refreshingly unpretentious and invariably packed, with all kinds of customers enjoying local seafood and wines. From inside the atmospheric restaurants, glimpses can be caught of the kitchens. Giant wooden fans in the ceiling waft in the smells. Señora Uti – amazingly fluent in English, Spanish, French and German – reserves special treatment for her hotel guests, and is generally to be found behind the bar.

The hotel itself is modern, behind an older five-storey moulded plaster frontage, the chief advantage being that inside it is clean and bright rather than notably well equipped. In the bedrooms you will find pleasant wooden furniture, firm beds, good views and plenty of space. Here there is no hint of the restaurant bustle. In addition, a small TV room with leather armchairs, dotted with antiques, ceramics and magazines, provides a quiet backwater, as does the small sun terrace, where you can be alone with the geraniums.

~

Nearby Main promenade and beach.
Location on seafront in centre of promenade; car parking (1,350 pesetas per 24 hours)
Meals breakfast, lunch, dinner
Prices rooms €€-€€€; buffet breakfast €; dinner €€, lunch €€
Rooms 63 double, 4 single, 3 family rooms, all with bath; all rooms have phone, minibar, safe, TV, air-conditioning, central heating
Facilities dining-room, sitting-room, bar
Credit cards AE, DC, MC, V
Children accepted
Disabled lift/elevator **Pets** small dogs accepted **Closed** Dec to Jan
Proprietor Antonìo Arcas

BARCELONA

TAVÉRNOLES

EL BANUS

~ COUNTRY GUEST-HOUSE ~

08519, Tavérnoles, Barcelona
TEL (93) 812 2091 **FAX** (93) 8887012
E-MAIL el-banus@netmail.es

The Banús family have farmed on this site since 1214, and have a stout family tree proudly displayed in their hall to prove it. The rambling soft-stone farmhouse is modern by comparison – construction started as late as the 15th century. Antonio Banús is still making improvements, with a little help from his son – gently converting an adjoining barn into a dining-room and adding a downstairs room and bathroom for disabled visitors. Meanwhile his wife prepares the solid four-course dinner with similarly traditional skill.

Meals are served in the pantry-cum-bar in front of an open fire (highly welcome in winter). The ample breakfasts are also taken here, with a choice of continental bread or pan con tomate y salchichon, a local speciality which Antonio insists is nothing like pizza. Rooms, on the second floor, are appropriately basic, with no en suite facilities (there are four shared bathrooms) and furnished with a suitably catholic collection of family heirlooms, some delightful. Two self-catering apartments for up to six people are also available. There is no midday meal, but the Banúses are more than happy to provide a picnic for those planning expeditions into the neighbouring foothills. The garden has some deliciously cool corners. According to a reader, some rooms are in need of attention. We would welcome more reports.

~

Nearby Vich (8 km); way-marked path to local sights.
Location in heart of open countryside near Vich PT; with garden and car parking
Meals breakfast, picnic lunches, dinner
Prices rooms ⓔ; breakfast ⓔ; dinner ⓔⓔ; discounts for children
Rooms 4 double, one family room; shared bathrooms; all rooms have central heating **Facilities** dining-room, sitting-room, bar; small swimming-pool, table tennis**Credit cards** AE, MC, V**Children** welcome **Disabled** one room on ground floor **Pets** well behaved dogs accepted
Closed one week in Sep **Proprietor** Antonio Banús

BARCELONA

VICH

PT DE VIC

~ MODERN PARADOR ~

Paraje el Bach de Sau, 08500, Vich, Barcelona
TEL (93) 8122323 **FAX** (93) 8122368

Isolated on a steep mountainside overlooking the expansive Sau reservoir, this Parador de Turismo is an imposing grey stone edifice. Completed in 1972 to mimic a Catalan farmhouse, it is quite wrong in scale, but it is nevertheless not without beauty. The conservatory-style entrance gives way to a vast galleried hall with murals, polished wooden pillars and a stained glass ceiling worthy of Chartres.

The sons and daughters from the masías dotted throughout the surrounding sierra have their wedding receptions here. Walkers and cyclists with sufficient energy come in search of a little luxury and a comfortable bed to rest their limbs. They are rarely disappointed. Rooms are furnished in classical Castilian or Catalan style. Those with larger bathrooms have the unusual luxury of double basins.

The dining-room is another large hall with mock-medieval chandeliers, marble pillars, and more murals. The three-course menu of international, Spanish and Catalan dishes is enhanced by the magnificent view, and as night falls the sounds of the wilderness outside add atmosphere to the occasion. The staff serve with appropriate hushed efficiency.

~

Nearby Vich (15 km); walks to nearby sights.
Location 14 km E of Vich, clearly signed from Vich; with gardens and parking for 30 cars
Meals breakfast, lunch, dinner
Prices rooms €€€-€€€€; breakfast €; meals €€
Rooms 29 double, 4 single, 1 suite, all with bath; all rooms have central heating, air-conditioning, phone, TV, minibar, safe
Facilities 2 sitting-rooms, bar, dining-room; tennis, swimming-pool
Credit cards AE, DC, MC, V
Children welcome
Disabled access easy; lift **Pets** accepted
Closed never
Manager Senor Puigdollers

GERONA

Hotels on the Costa Brava

The 'Spanish Riviera' has emerged over the past 30 years as the Costa del Sol's major competitor for Spain's holiday trade. But, unlike the Costa del Sol, it is a naturally rugged coastline of rocky coves, sandy beaches, pine-clad cliffs and little fishing villages. For high season, book well in advance.

Blanes, the 'official' starting point of the Costa Brava, has many inexpensive hotels, pensions and campsites along one of the Costa's longest beaches. Lloret de Mar boasts an even longer beach and a even greater concentration of hotels, restaurants and nightclubs. If you want some solitude, try the 80-room family-owned Santa Marta (Tel (972) 364904), down a winding driveway in an area of private villas and botanical gardens. It is renowned for its seafood, eaten on the terrace overlooking the beach. Tossa de Mar has several smart little hotels, including one which merits a detailed description (page 82). The 74-room S'Agaró Hotel (Tel (972) 325200) is a good second best in S'Agaró after the luxurious La Gavina (page 88). North of the Palafrugell area (which has an abundance of places to stay) are many smaller resorts with some reasonable (but not notable) hotels.

READERS' REPORTS

Please write and tell us about your experiences of small hotels, guest-houses and inns, whether good or bad, whether listed in this edition or not. As well as hotels in Spain, we are interested in hotels in Britain and Ireland, Italy, France, Portugal, Austria, Switzerland, Germany and other European countries, and those in the eastern United States.

The address to write to is:

The Editor,
Charming Small Hotel Guides,
c/o Duncan Petersen Publishing Ltd,
31 Ceylon Road,
London W14 OPY.

To the hundreds of readers who have written with comments on hotels in all the *Charming Small Hotel Guides*, a sincere 'thank-you'. We attach great importance to your comments and absorb them into the text each year. Please keep writing: for further information see page 12.

GERONA

TOSSA DE MAR

HOTEL DIANA

SEASIDE HOTEL

Plaza d'España 6, 17320, Tossa de Mar, Gerona
TEL (972) 341886 **FAX** (972) 341103

After the castle, the Hotel Diana is architecturally one of the most important buildings in Tossa. A family town house built on the central Plaza d'Espana in the 1850s, and backing on to the main promenade, it became a hotel a hundred years later. Today, when it opens for the summer season, it attracts an international clientele of art-nouveau-lovers.

The entire building is a tribute to the period, with a Gaudi roof faced with characteristic broken turquoise tiles, stained glass windows, a sweeping marble staircase and original Gaudi fireplace. The central salon contains art-nouveau frescoes, which have recently been restored, and a bronze fountain in naked female form by the Catalan sculptor Mares; light streams in through the glass roof three storeys above. The bedrooms are set in the surrounding gallery. With their high arched ceilings, marble floors and grand wooden shutters, they have plenty to offer in terms of style. Breakfast is taken either on the sea-front terrace or in the inner courtyard.

In 1989, after a period on lease, the Diana was returned to its original owners, a local hotel-owning family, who are continuing to carry out extensive refurbishment.

Nearby Castle; promenade; central beach.
Location entrance on Plaza d'España, rear entrance on beach promenade; no private car parking
Meals breakfast
Prices rooms €€-€€€; breakfast €P
Rooms 20 double, one single, all with bath; all rooms have TV, phone, minibar; some with sea views
Facilities sitting-room, TV room,bar
Credit cards AE, MC, V **Children** welcome
Disabled access easy; lift/elevator
Pets accepted **Closed** Oct to May
Manager Fernando Osorio

GERONA

AIGUA BLAVA

HOTEL AIGUA BLAVA

~ SEASIDE HOTEL ~

Playa de Fornells, 17255, Aigua Blava, Gerona
TEL (972) 622058 **FAX** (972) 622112

Too big to include in the guide but too distinctive to leave out, the Aigua Blava is a holiday village with a difference – a collection of delightful annexes among shady, pine-covered cliffs and flowered terraces, set round a tiny fishing harbour and beach, the whole arrangement is the opus of multi-lingual ex-swimming champion, Xiquet Sabater – a man whose life history would defy belief if it were not confirmed in the Spanish Who's Who?

The complex provides everything you need, even a boutique complete with genuine French assistance. Each room has individual style, ranging from summerhouse brightness in some annexes to the more formal bedrooms in the main hotel. Even the least inspiring are immaculate, and the sea views are out of this world. Guests who reserve a table in the pleasant terrace restaurant are rewarded with a feast of a four-course meal, with plenty of choice and desserts ranging from the holy to the sinful.

This area has always been Xiquet's home, and he wants his guests to feel the same warmth as if it were theirs, too. If the four generations who come back to this Mediterranean idyll year after year (making early booking essential) are any guide, he succeeds – with abundant help from his cheerful staff.

~

Nearby Bagur (5 km); beach.
Location in quiet spot near beach; with gardens and car parking
Meals breakfast, lunch, dinner
Prices rooms €€€€; breakfast €; meals €€ **Rooms** 64 double, 8 single, 14 suites, 2 family rooms, all with bath; all rooms have central heating, phone; most rooms have air-conditioning **Facilities** 4 dining-rooms, 4 sitting-rooms, 2 bars; swimming-pool, tennis courts, volley ball
Credit cards AE, DC, MC, V
Children welcome; play area **Disabled** no special facilities
Pets small dogs accepted
Closed Nov to end Feb **Manager** Juan Gispert

GERONA

CASTELLO DE AMPURIAS

HOTEL ALLIOLI
∾ COUNTRY INN ∾

Urbanización Castellonou 17486, Castelló de Ampurias, Gerona
TEL (972) 250320 **FAX** (972) 250300

The setting for this country inn, in a dusty basin below the main Roses-Figueras road, could be better. But it could also be much worse: the neighbouring blue and white-washed Danone plant is almost picturesque as factories go. And the building itself more than makes up for its surroundings: a two-hundred-year-old Catalan farmhouse of considerable character.

Inside, the Peig Callol family have sympathetically fitted it out with antiques, lamps and benches, spiced up with fresh and dried flowers. Huge, whole dried Jamon Jabugos hams hang over the intimate bar to dry. The bedrooms display pure rural simplicity with linen counterpanes, exposed beams and whitewashed walls. But there are creature comforts too: clean en suite bathrooms, plenty of gadgets, and well-placed electric lights. The beamed four-chambered restaurant is well suited to the vast feasts local Spanish families come to devour on a Sunday. During the week Maria Callol will serve you a quieter, but no less sumptuous Catalan meal, or even paella. Breakfast on the patio can be a very pleasant experience, provided the seasonal winds don't blow away your croissant. On such occasions, the bar is a safer alternative. Visitors to Allioli wrote that they were 'charmed'.

∾

Nearby Figueras (10 km); Rosas (8 km)
Location in grounds set back from main Figueras/Roses road; with car parking
Meals breakfast, lunch, dinner
Prices rooms €€-€€€; breakfast €; dinner €€
Rooms 31 double, 8 single, all with bath; all rooms have central heating, air-conditioning, phone, TV **Facilities** 2 dining-rooms, 2 sitting-rooms, bar
Credit cards MC, V
Children accepted **Disabled** lift/elevator **Pets** accepted in rooms
Closed 23 Dec to 10 Feb
Proprietor José Peig Rions and Maria Callol

GERONA

GERONA

HOSTAL BELLMIRALL
~ TOWN GUEST-HOUSE ~

Calle Bellmirall 3, 17000, Gerona
TEL (972) 204009

Anna Pascual and Isidre Vicens run this diminutive guest-house, hidden away just to the right of the cathedral steps, as a family home, which it is. The house is a 14thC historic monument of ancient stone, which Anna and Isidre started converting to take guests in the 60s; they continue to make minor adjustments to this day. Isidre is supposedly the artist of the family, and his paintings, and those of Catalan colleagues, line the walls, and are displayed in a small gallery; his studio is on the top floor. But Anna's artistry is plain in the interior design which is all highly individual (the brightly decorated breakfast room and hand-made bedspreads are a joy), and in the breakfasts, which are also something special.

Anna and Isidre serve no other meals, though they offer the occasional beer, and advise (at length) on where to eat in the town. Breakfast is served on the pretty patio. Service is highly personal, but this is not a hotel. Rooms have few en suite facilities and visitors who demand to see them before checking in risk being turned away. Anna and Isidre are busy enough with their satisfied regulars, and do not advertise. Indeed, it took an hour of pleading over a beer to elicit the information we needed for an entry here.

~

Nearby Cathedral; museums; old Gerona.
Location in tiny street next to cathedral; no private parking
Meals breakfast
Prices €€€-€€€€ with breakfast
Rooms 3 double, 2 with shower; 2 single, one with shower; 2 family rooms, both with shower
Facilities sitting-room, breakfast room, patio
Credit cards not accepted
Children welcome **Disabled** no special facilities **Pets** not accepted
Closed 15 Nov 1 Mar
Proprietor Anna Pascual and Isidre Vicens

GERONA

PALAFRUGELL

HOTEL LLEVANT

～ SEASIDE HOTEL ～

Francesc de Blanes 5, 17200, Llafranc, Palafrugell, Gerona
TEL (972) 300366 **FAX** (972) 300345

This unassuming three-storey house, right on the main promenade of the surprisingly unspoilt fishing village of Llafranc, was a restaurant before the Spanish Civil War. It had only six rooms when Jaume Farrarons took it over. Since then the family have built it up, and now they feel enough is enough, though they are planning a few minor improvements. Food is their true love, and heaven forbid that the hotel should start to overshadow the restaurant.

For the time being, at least, they have no need to worry: the Llevant's individual French-influenced Catalan cuisine draws a discerning crowd at all times of year. The excellent fish dishes are much enhanced by the sea air and sophisticated French café-style surroundings. The four-course menu will leave you staggering for a comfortable chair, which you will find without difficulty on the covered terrace adjoining, or in the small salon where exhibitions of local art are regularly housed.

If you are not up to the similarly proportioned buffet breakfasts of cheese and charcuterie, then a Continental breakfast can be taken in the bedrooms, which are simple but airy and tasteful.

～

Nearby Palafrugell (4 km); coastal walks; beach and harbour.
Location on main promenade in heart of village; no private car parking
Meals breakfast, lunch, dinner
Prices rooms €€€-€€€€; breakfast €; meals €€
Rooms 22 double, 18 with bath, 4 with shower, 6 single, 2 with wash-basin, 2 with shower, 2 with bath; all rooms have central heating, TV; 18 rooms have air-conditioning
Facilities dining-room, sitting-room, bar, terrace
Credit cards MC, V
Children welcome
Disabled access difficult **Pets** accepted in rooms
Closed Nov to 15 Dec; restaurant only, Sun night Jan to Mar
Proprietor Jaume Farrarons

GERONA

PALAFRUGELL

HOTEL SANT ROC

～ SEASIDE HOTEL ～

Pl del Atlántico, 2, Calella de Palafrugell, 17210, Palafrugell, Gerona
TEL (972) 614250/615286 **FAX** (972) 614068/617012

High on the cliffs of Calella de Palafrugell, with magnificent views from the leafy terrace over the bay and steps down to the shore, the Sant Roc started life as a family home in the 1950s but was soon converted to an hotel, and has been expanded since. It is an appealing building, in style somewhere between a grand Catalan country house and a mini-monastery, featuring a terracotta roofed tower.

It aims to be a family-run hotel run for families; guests are treated like old friends, and some return to the Sant Roc year after year. The interior is stylish, but pleasantly lived in. The wicker rocking chairs and antiques are there to be used, as is the more utilitarian furniture. You might find the wallpaper peeling in those rooms that are next on the list for re-furbishment, and not all of them have sea views, but they are clean, with original oil paintings on the walls and traditional Catalan wooden furniture painted in red, green or blue, known as polycromodo.

The three-course dinner and lunch menu has three choices for starter and main-course, and there is always the *carte* in the panoramic restaurant.

～

Nearby Calella (0.3 km); Palafrugell (4 km); beach.
Location on cliffs, set back from road amid trees; with garden and car parking
Meals breakfast, lunch, dinner
Prices rooms ©©-©©©; breakfast ©, dinner ©©
Rooms 40 double, 1 single, 5 suites, 1 family room, all with bath; all have central heating, some with air-conditioning, phone, TV, safe
Facilities dining-room, sitting-room, bar, terrace; table tennis
Credit cards AE, DC, MC, V
Children welcome; baby-sitting available
Disabled lift/elevator; ground-floor rooms
Pets accepted in rooms
Closed 10 Nov to 15 Mar
Manager Teresa Boix

GERONA

S'AGARO

HOSTAL DE LA GAVINA

~ SEASIDE HOTEL ~

Plaza de la Rosaleda, 17248, S'Agaró, Gerona
TEL (972) 321100 **FAX** (972) 321573
E-MAIL gavina@iponet.es **WEBSITE** www.iponet.es\gavina

Set in secluded grounds on the edge of S'Agaró, above a small beach (with brightly painted huts, straight out of a 1930s musical, where the rich and famous rub sun-burnt shoulders with the merely affluent), this majestic Catalan villa is reminiscent of the great palaces of Europe, except that it is better cared for. A full description of the furnishings would read like a Christie's catalogue; as you wander through the circular formation of marbled salons and halls, the eye is met by enticing clusters of antique furniture, making it impossible to decide whether to continue or sit down. The immaculate bedrooms are all individually furnished in the style of your choice – Regency, rich walnut, Catalan polycromodo.

Not all is elegance. The 'El Barco' bar is, as its name suggests, built like the inside of a wooden boat. There are two restaurants, both serving the same Catalan/modern Spanish carte – one in French brasserie style, the other candle-lit, in plush Regency style – jacket and tie required.

Run by the son of the man who built it, the place is surprisingly relaxed for somewhere so opulent. The only thing to deter most people is the price.

~

Nearby Sant Feliu de Guíxols (4 km); beach.
Location above beach on edge of main S'Agaró development; with gardens, and garaging for 14 cars and car parking
Meals breakfast, lunch, dinner
Prices rooms €€€€€; breakfast €€; meals €€€
Rooms 55 double, 2 single, 16 suites, all with bath; all rooms have phone, TV, radio, minibar, hairdrier
Facilities 2 dining-rooms, sitting-rooms, bar, gymnasium, sauna, jacuzzi, terrace; sea- water pool, tennis courts
Credit cards AE, DC, MC, V
Children accepted **Disabled** access easy; ground-floor rooms; lift/elevator
Pets accepted in bedrooms **Closed** Nov to Mar
Manager Ana Requena

GERONA

HOTEL HOSTALILLO

∾ SEASIDE HOTEL ∾

Bellavista 22, 17212, Tamariú, Gerona
TEL (972) 620228 **FAX** (972) 620184

This modern hotel is lifted out of the Costa rut by attention to detail and its tranquil location. Staff are friendly, efficient and helpful, the atmosphere welcoming – the hotel feels much smaller than its rule-breaking number of rooms would at first suggest.

Even from the outside, the Hostalillo is more than usually appealing: the five storeys are set into the steep hillside and pitched terracotta roofs help to break up the lines of the concrete.

The white walls inside give a cool, airy feel. The large split-level dining-room is flexible enough not to seem bare, even in low season. Here the four-course menu (constantly varied, with plenty of choice) can be struggled through, overlooking the inviting sun terrace full of geraniums and simple, comfortable chairs. Below is the once-picturesque fishing village of Tamariú, where the boats on the beach still out-number the frying bodies except in July and August. Steps lead through the garden, down the cliffs to the beach.

Bedrooms have all you can expect from a sound, basic beach hotel, including a view of the bay or the mountains.

∾

Nearby Palafrugell (4 km); coastal walks; beach.
Location on cliffs above village, overlooking Tamariú; with garden and parking for 13 cars
Meals breakfast, dinner
Prices rooms €€€-€€€€€; breakfast €; dinner €€
Rooms 59 double, 2 single, 3 family rooms, 6 suites, all with bath; all rooms have phone; most rooms have central heating
Facilities dining-room, sitting/TV room, bar
Credit cards AE, MC, V
Children accepted **Disabled** access difficult **Pets** accepted
Closed 20 Sep to 1 May
Manager José M Biarge

GERONA

VILADRAU

HOSTAL DE LA GLORIA

~ COUNTRY HOTEL ~

Torreventosa 12, 08553, Viladrau, Gerona
TEL (93) 884 9034 **FAX** (93) 884 9465

This cosy country lodge was built over 50 years ago in simple Catalan style. Set just above the pleasant mountain village of Viladrau, with a pretty, peaceful garden terrace in front and the Sierra rising behind, it is a favourite with ageing Spanish card-players, who fill the inter-connecting small salons and leatherette armchairs at weekends throughout the year.

The Formatje family have decked the place out with copper pots, brass lamps, paintings and some fine old Spanish chairs, and keep the whole spotlessly clean. They are proud of their hostal, always eager to please, and genuinely apologetic when their rooms are full.

Rooms are simple and old-fashioned, with modern bathrooms. The four-course lunch and dinner menus are different each day, and are highly recommended. They are served in an attractive arched dining-room with a pretty tiled floor, wooden beams, green lace curtains and white walls hand-painted with birds and decorated with plates.

Overall, the result is an unpretentious home from home, where relaxation comes naturally – aided by the knowledge that rooms and meals are notably cheap.

~

Nearby Gerona (60 km); Vich (25 km); Montseny Sierra.
Location above mountain village in Sierra de Montseny; with covered car park
Meals breakfast, lunch, dinner
Prices rooms €€-€€€; breakfast €; meals €€
Rooms 20 double, 3 single, one suite, 2 family rooms, all with bath; all rooms have central heating, phone, TV
Facilities dining-room, sitting-room, bar, swimming-pool
Credit cards MC, V
Children accepted
Disabled no special facilities
Pets not accepted
Closed 22 Dec to 7 Jan
Proprietors Eudald Formatje

GERONA

FIGUERAS

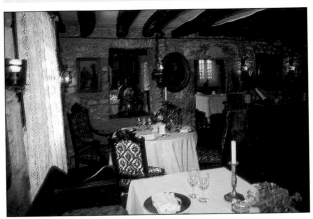

MAS PAU

～ COUNTRY HOTEL ～

Avinyonet de Puigventós, 17742, Figueras, Gerona
TEL (972) 546154

This creeper-covered family-run hotel is a converted 17thC masia (a large, well-to-do farmhouse) standing by itself in wooded and farmed countryside near the village of Figueras (made famous by Salvador Dalí). It has been run by Nuria Serrat and her family since the 70s and, wedding parties permitting, you can be certain of friendly personal service.

The public rooms are essentially rustic, but decorated in modernista style, the Spanish equivalent of art nouveau. They include an arched bar (with painted mirrors, vases of ferns, wicker chairs around tables made from old sewing machines), and three interconnecting dining-rooms. The largest of these, the banqueting room, has a beamed ceiling and stone walls covered in old photos of Figueras. The seven suites look out on to tranquil gardens and cypress trees. They are decorated entirely in pink and grey; grey carpets, pink marble bath-rooms and – according to Señora Serrat – curtains and bedspreads that change with the seasons: warm pink in winter, cool grey in summer.

In the well established gardens is a modest but attractive pool, with a shaded terrace on hand.

～

Nearby Figueras – Dali museum; Gerona (40 km).
Location in countryside, 4 km SW of village of Figueras; with garden and car parking
Meals breakfast, lunch, dinner
Prices rooms €€€-€€€€; breakfast €; meals from €€
Rooms 12 suites, all with bath; all rooms have central heating, phone, TV, air-conditioning, minibar
Facilities dining-room, sitting-room, bar, banquet/conference room, terrace; swimming-pool
Credit cards AE, DC, MC, V
Children welcome; playground
Disabled easy access; some ground-floor rooms
Pets dogs accepted **Closed** never; restaurant only, Sun in winter
Proprietor Nuria Serrat

GERONA

TORRENT

HOTEL MAS DE TORRENT
⌁ COUNTRY HOUSE HOTEL ⌁

Afores s/n, 17123, Torrent, Gerona
TEL (972) 303292 **FAX** (972) 303293
E-MAIL mtorrent@intercom.es **WEBSITE** www.mastorrent.com

The setting of this stunning conversion of a 1751 Catalan *masia* is truly superb: in lush grounds concealing extensive terraces, pelota, paddle-ball and tennis courts, and the inevitable swimming-pool, amid open countryside, with views over Pals to the castle at Bagur beyond.

Just when you have come to terms with the exterior, you are confronted by further splendour inside. The style of the original interior is faithfully reproduced, but with a layer of luxury applied with impeccable taste. A series of arched salons with bright sofas and a fireplace gives way to the bar and terraces. Upstairs there are further spacious salons, with huge sofas and antiques, around which the individually named and styled rooms are set. 'Las Hortensias' is all antiques and lace, for example, while 'Las Dacias' is pure Barcelona chic. The 20 rooms in the garden bungalows have private, hedged terraces and more of a summerhouse feel. All are faultless in terms of facilities.

The dining-room which adjoins the main building is an impressive reproduction, with the exposed roof beams and slates typical of the region. There is an extravagant four-course menu and seasonal carte of Catalan, Basque and French cuisine.

Nearby Pals (4 km); Costa Brava beaches (14 km).
Location near tiny village; with garden, car parking
Meals breakfast, lunch, dinner
Prices rooms €€€€€; breakfast €€, meals €€€
Rooms 32 double, all with bath; all rooms have central heating, air-conditioning, phone, TV, minibar, radio, hairdrier, safe
Facilities dining-room, 4 sitting-rooms, games room; swimming-pool, tennis court **Credit cards** AE, DC, MC, V **Children** accepted;
Disabled access easy; specially adapted room and other ground-floor rooms
Pets accepted (extra charge) **Closed** never
Manager Gregorio Berengüí

GERONA

TORRE DEL REMEI
~ TOWN HOTEL ~

Camí Reial s/n, 17463, Bolvir de Cerdanya, Gerona
TEL (972) 140182

With considerable effort and impeccable taste, José María Boix and his wife, Loles Vidal, turned the Boix in Martinet into one of the most renowned restaurant-cum-hotels in the Catalan Pyrenees, and one of the top ten restaurants in Spain. Now they are repeating their success with this sumptuous mansion a short way from Puigcerdá.

The house, a colonial caprice of the belle époque, was built in 1910 and has been equipped as a luxury hotel by some of the most imaginative designers in Catalonia. The marble is from Greece; the furniture from Italy; the carpets from Tibet. Outside there is a 20,000 square metre garden planted with firs, towering redwoods, a swimming-pool and a putting green.

The Boix have created an oasis of elegance: expensive details abound – Bang & Olufsen video and TV, the selection of Loewe perfumes served by a valet. You will not lack creature comforts: the bathroom floors are heated and the king-size baths have hydromassage.

As you would expect, the cooking is also imaginative and appetizing. But the core of the appeal is most appreciated is the personal service that José María and Loles offer their guests.
~

Nearby S Domingo church; walls, town hall of Puigcerdá (3 km).
Location in the outskirts of Puigcerdá; garden and car parking
Meals breakfast, lunch, dinner
Prices rooms €€€€; breakfast €€; meals €€€
Rooms 4 double, 7 suites all with bath; all rooms have hydromassage, central heating, telephone, video, TV (satellite)
Facilities dining-room, video library, private meeting room; swimming-pool, putting green **Credit cards** AE, DC, MC, V
Children welcome **Disabled** no special facilities; lift/elevator
Pets accepted in bedrooms **Closed** never
Proprietor José María Boix and Loles Vidal

ZAMORA

BENAVENTE

PT REY FERNANDO II DE LEON
~ CASTLE PARADOR ~

Paseo Ramón y Cajal s/n, 49600, Benavente, Zamora
TEL (980) 630300 **FAX** (980) 638303

One look at the extraordinary sitting-room and you will probably excuse whatever shortcomings this hotel has. This voluminous hall occupies most of the old castle keep, the Tower of the Snail (the only part of the original building which was not destroyed by the French in the last century), which stands on a prominent cliff a short way out of town. Deep corner alcoves penetrate the turrets to reach snug stone benches by sunny windows. Large old tapestries adorn the walls. Overhead is a magnificent Mudejar coffered ceiling which was taken from a church.

A worn stone staircase (straight out of The Name of the Rose) takes you to another striking chamber below – the second bar, open only in the evenings – which has 2-metre thick walls, an enormous circular iron chandelier and some extremely interesting old furnishings.

The rest of the hotel, however, is modern and characterless in comparison. The dining-room and smaller bar have brick arches and a wall of windows giving views of fertile agricultural plains (shame about the flour mill immediately below). Twenty of the rooms have balconies sharing the same view.

~

Nearby Zamora (65 km); León (69 km); Puebla de Sanabria (84 km).
Location on hill overlooking town; with garden and car parking
Meals breakfast, lunch, dinner
Prices rooms €€€€-€€€€€; breakfast €; meals €€
Rooms 28 double, 2 single, all with bath; all rooms have
central heating, air-conditioning, phone,
TV, minibar
Facilities dining-room, sitting-room, 2 bars, TV room
Credit cards AE, DC, MC, V
Children welcome **Disabled** access easy; 9 ground-floor rooms
Pets not accepted **Closed** never
Manager Concepción Lechuga

ZAMORA

La Hostería Real de Zamora

~ Historic palace ~

Cuesta de Pizarro, 7, 49001, Zamora
Tel (980) 534545 **Fax** (980) 5353
E-mail host.zamora@wanadoo.es

Opened in 1990, the hotel occupies a 16thC palace next to an old stone bridge over the Duero, beside the city walls. The building was once the home of the Spanish Inquisition. A former inhabitant was Francisco Pizarro, discoverer of Peru.

The Hostería offers a remarkable amount of comfort for the age of the building, making it a reasonable alternative to the nearby Parador. Of special note is its beautiful claustral patio. The restaurant, adjacent to the old city walls, specializes in regional food with a strong Basque bias.

~

Nearby Romanesque churches; Gothic altarpiece, Arcenillas (6 km); 7thC Visigothic church, near El Campillo (20 km).
Location beside the ring-road connecting the roads to Galicia, Salamanca and Portugal; garden and car parking outside
Meals breakfast, lunch, dinner **Prices** rooms €€; breakfast €; meals €€
Rooms 13 double, 2 single, one family, all with bath; all rooms have telephone, safe, minibar, radio, TV (satellite) **Facilities** restaurant, meeting rooms, cafeteria
Credit cards AE, DC, MC, V **Children** welcome
Disabled access easy to rooms 101 and 102
Pets accepted **Closed** never **Manager** Yolanda Fidalgo

PARADORES IN WESTERN SPAIN

THE PROVINCES OF ZAMORA AND SALAMANCA (around the NE corner of Portugal) have several pleasant Paradores which are described in detail in this section. In addition, Salamanca's modern white Parador sits on a hill above the town, traditionally the site of one of Castille's biggest cattle fairs. The best we can say about the hotel is that every guest room has a superb view of the town at night. Rooms are adequate and have sliding doors leading to small 'galleries' furnished with cane chairs (Tel (923) 192082).

The further south you travel, the fewer and further between Paradores become. The harsh terrain of Extremadura has kept the developers out from Roman times onwards, and only recently (and with a lot of funding from the EC, drawn to your attention on huge billboards at regular intervals) has the area been opened up by an extensive network of new roads. The existing Paradores, now more accessible, are all in ancient buildings – converted monasteries (Trujillo, Guadalupe, Mérida), hilltop castles (Oropesa, Jarandilla, Zafra) and a 14thC town house at Cáceres. Most have detailed entries. Two Paradores in splendid castles have recently undergone extensive renovation – one in an imposing 15thC fortress in the middle of Zafra (Tel (924) 554540) and the PT Virrey de Toledo, perched above the little town of Oropesa (Tel (925) 430000).

ZAMORA

ZAMORA

PT CONDES DE ALBA Y ALISTE

∽ PALACE PARADOR ∽

Plaza Viriato 5, 49001, Zamora
TEL (980) 514497 **FAX** (980) 530063
E-MAIL zamora@parador.es

Zamora may seem out of the way for most visitors, but here is a hotel worth the detour. Much less interfered with than other Paradors occupying historic buildings, this palace surrounds a photogenic Renaissance courtyard fringed with carved stone pillars. The sunny enclosed halls and balconies along the four sides of the courtyard are decorated with antiques and pot plants (there are even plants sprouting out of an antique chest).

Many of the furnishings are original, or at least apt; the tarnished-green dining-room chandeliers have stags fleeing from their hubs. And at the foot of the stairs a complete suit of armour for a knight and his horse is on display. Most of the bedrooms have an old-fashioned feel; that is, they don't feel anonymously modern, but the number of rooms has doubled since our last edition. Some of them have double-doored windows opening on to the swimming-pool, others have canopied double beds, while the six suites available are as large as apartments.

The swimming-pool is open to the public, making this Parador feel less privileged than most others, particularly at weekends, when the pool can be busy (and noisy).

∽

Nearby Romanesque churches; Gothic altarpiece, Arcenillas (6 km); 7thC Visigothic church, near El Campillo (20 km).
Location in main square; with garden and car parking
Meals breakfast, lunch, dinner
Prices rooms €€€€-€€€€€; breakfast €; dinner €€
Rooms 52 doubles, 6 suites, all with bath; all rooms have central heating, phone, TV, minibar
Facilities dining-room, 2 sitting-rooms, bar, terrace; swimming-pool (public)
Credit cards AE, DC, MC, V
Children welcome **Disabled** easy access; lift/elevator **Pets** accepted **Closed** never
Manager Pilar Pelegrin

SALAMANCA

CIUDAD RODRIGO

HOTEL CONDE RODRIGO

~ CITY HOTEL ~

Plaza de San Salvador 9, 37500, Ciudad Rodrigo, Salamanca
TEL (923) 461404 **FAX** (923) 48108

THE CONDE RODRIGO OCCUPIES A HANDSOME 16thC stone-built palace on a leafy, historic square. It has, unfortunately, been insensitively modernized inside, obviously with the best of intentions. The bedrooms, though adequate, lack character but they offer some surprise extras, such as shoe-brushes in the bathrooms. It is popular for family functions, when the sitting-room is converted into a rowdy banqueting hall. There is also a disco in the basement. The restaurant serves a varied and economical menu. A sister hotel, Conde Rodrigo II, just out of town, is unashamedly modern, with its own pool and tennis court.

~

NEARBY Plaza Mayor (short walk); Portugal (30 km).
LOCATION in square in historic centre, signed from Salamanca road; with small car parking area
MEALS breakfast, lunch, dinner
PRICES rooms €-€€; breakfast €; menu €
MEALS 50 double with bath, 4 single with shower; all rooms have central heating, phone, TV, minibar, radio
FACILITIES sitting-room, dining- room, bar, terrace, disco
CREDIT CARDS AE, DC, MC, V **CHILDREN** Welcome **DISABLED** access easy
PETS not accepted **CLOSED** never **MANAGER** Ceferino Santos

LA ALBERCA

Las Batuecas

~ Country hotel ~

Carretera Las Batuecas, 37624, La Alberca, Salamanca
Tel (923) 415188 **Fax** (923) 415055
E-mail lasbatuecas@teleline.es

A popular weekend destination for Madrileuños, Las Batuecas is an imposing stone building located on the edge of the quaint village of La Alberca, in the heart of the fascinating Sierra de Francia, with its chestnut-woods and picturesque terraces of cherry-trees. The hotel begins on the first floor with a wide, covered terrace. Behind is a garden with a lawn and rose-clad trellis, and the rest of the floor is an open-plan lounge-bar-dining-room. The bedrooms and bathrooms have recently been refurbished and the windows sealed against the cold. A useful base for walking, cycling or touring.

~

Nearby La Alberca; Las Batuecas scenic road (40 km trip).
Location in village; withgarden and car parking
Meals breakfast, lunch, dinner
Prices rooms €€; breakfast €; meals €-€€
Rooms 22 double, 2 single, 3 family rooms, all with bath; all rooms have central heating, phone, TV, minibar
Facilities sitting-room, dining-room, bar, terrace
Credit cards MC, V **Children** welcome **Disabled** access difficult
Pets accepted only in bedrooms **Closed** Jan to Mar
Manager Augustina Puerto

SALAMANCA

CIUDAD RODRIGO

PT ENRIQUE II

~ CASTLE PARADOR ~

Plaza del Castillo 1, 37500, Ciudad Rodrigo, Salamanca
TEL (923) 460150 **FAX** (923) 460404

Don't be disappointed if what you thought was the hotel – a stout tower with battlements – turns out to be only a warehouse. The hotel itself is the low-lying, attractively ivy-clad building beneath it. This was the second Parador to be opened, and the first to occupy a historic building. Fortunately, the present manager has paid more personal attention to it than many of those running other castles in the state hotel chain, and is still continuing to make improvements.

The rooms are spread out along two wings – one ancient, one modern. The former are reached by an arched curving white corridor; the 'star' is Room 10, a suite in which the bedroom is circular with a domed roof. Four of the rooms abut the old city walls and have views over the hotel's formal gardens. The public areas are decorated with occasional antiques, some suits of armour and plenty of green pot plants. The dining-room and sitting-room are both attractive, with partially sloping ceilings and wide basket-handle stone arches.

For pure history and a great view, don't forget to climb the tower. It is reached through the castle's original gate (ask for the key from reception), now in a splendid, crumbling state.

~

Nearby Plaza Mayor; Portugal (30 km); La Alberca (50 km).
Location on a quiet open square near centre of town; with garden and car parking
Meals breakfast, lunch, dinner
Prices rooms ⓔⓔⓔ-ⓔⓔⓔⓔ; breakfast ⓔ; dinner ⓔⓔ
Rooms 26 double, 1 suite, all with bath; all rooms have central heating, phone, TV, minibar
Facilities dining-room, 2 sitting-rooms, bar, patio
Credit cards AE, DC, MC, V
Children welcome; 20% discount for children under 10
Disabled access difficult **Pets** not accepted **Closed** never
Manager Angel Aliste

CACERES

GUADALUPE

PT ZURBARAN

~ CONVERTED HOSPICE ~

Marqués de la Romana 12, 10140, Guadalupe, Cáceres
TEL (927) 367075 **FAX** (927) 367076
E-MAIL guadalupe@parador.es

Named after the 17thC painter, this Parador started life as a hospice in the 14thC, housing pilgrims who had come to venerate the Black Virgin of Guadalupe. The road through the hills has probably not improved much since their day, but the spectacular views of mountains and valleys – and of Guadalupe – make up for the hairpin bends and pot-holes.

The Parador is a simple, whitewashed building, centred around an open cobbled courtyard full of orange trees, with dozens of peculiar domed chimney-pots on its red-tiled roofs. Low arched doorways in the cloisters lead to a sitting-room on one side and a wood-beamed bar on the other. The dining-room, on the third side of the quadrangle, looks out through French windows on to lovely gardens. In summer, tables are set on the terrace, so you can eat and drink overlooking a water-garden and tiled pavilion beyond.

The modern concrete annexe of twenty bedrooms overlooks the gardens and swimming-pool. Rooms here are more spacious than those in the old part and all have balconies. But they do lack character, and it is always the original rooms that sell out.

~

Nearby 14thC Franciscan monastery (Zurbarán's paintings), mountain passes and surrounding countryside.
Location opposite Franciscan Monastery, in middle of town; with garden and garage
Meals breakfast, lunch, dinner
Prices rooms €€-€€€€; breakfast €; meals €€
Rooms 40 double, all with bath; all rooms have central heating, phone, TV, minibar, radio; most rooms have air-conditioning
Facilities 2 dining-rooms, sitting-room, bar; swimming-pool, tennis court
Credit cards AE, DC, MC, V **Children** welcome
Disabled ground-floor rooms; lift/elevator
Pets accepted but not in dining-room **Closed** never
Manager José Manuel Piña

CÁCERES

GUADALUPE

HOSPEDERIA DEL REAL MONASTERIO

~ CONVERTED MONASTERY ~

Plaza Juan Carlos 1, 10140, Guadalupe, Cáceres
TEL (927) 367000 **FAX** (927) 367177

The Hospedería is part of a 16thC monastery, which dominates the Guadalupe skyline. It is still a working monastery; Franciscan brothers live in one half of the building, guests in the other.

The bedrooms are set around a magnificent stone-arcaded courtyard. Many of them are the original monks' cells – long narrow rooms with high ceilings and low stone doorways. They are all different; some very elaborate, some very basic. On one side there is an exquisite suite full of ornate antiques, on the other, simple single rooms.

The public rooms downstairs are equally original; the sombre sitting-room contrasts with a cheerful white dining-room, with fresh flowers on every table. There is also a TV room arranged like a cinema, and an inviting bar with an arched roof and marble floor. Tables are set out in the charming courtyard.

Although we arrived in the middle of a wedding reception for two hundred guests, the staff were not remotely put out and could not have been more helpful – the monks even gave us a guided tour of the monastery. 'Wow' says an American reader who recently stayed in 15 hotels in the guide: 'the nicest place we stayed in and probably the best bargain in the book.'

~

Nearby 14thC Franciscan monastery (Zurbarán's paintings); mountain passes and surrounding countryside.
Location within monastery, entrance up a flight of steps from main road; parking for 30 cars
Meals breakfast, lunch, dinner
Prices rooms €-€€; breakfast €; meals €€
Rooms 40 double, one single, 5 family rooms, one suite, all with bath; all rooms have central heating, phone; some rooms have air-conditioning
Facilities dining-room, sitting-room, TV room, bar
Credit cards MC, V **Children** welcome **Disabled** ground-floor rooms, lift/elevator
Pets not accepted**Closed** Jan 15 to Feb 15 **Manager** Fray Juan Luis Barrera

CÁCERES

JARANDILLA DE LA VERA

PT CARLOS V

~ CONVERTED CASTLE ~

Avda García, Prieto 1, 10450, Jarandilla de la Vera, Cáceres
Tel (927) 560117 **Fax** (927) 560088
E-MAIL jarandilla@parador.es

An imposing 15thC castle on the edge of a little white town makes a perfect setting for a Parador – which is why the Carlos V is often fully booked. The Parador architects have modernized it without losing any of its medieval flavour; it is difficult to tell that the new extension is not part of the original building. An arched doorway between round towers leads into a cobbled courtyard. Small shuttered windows peep out of cold grey walls and an arcaded balcony looks down from solid square towers.

Most of the public rooms are simply furnished in a modern style. Sombre oil paintings hang on the walls of the upstairs sitting-room, which opens on to the balcony set with yellow and white chairs. The bar and dining-room are bright and comfortable, and look on to the Parador gardens. The original bedrooms lead off tall, narrow, beamed corridors and have all the usual facilities. Rooms in the extension are light and spacious.

There is plenty to do outside; for the energetic, a swimming-pool and tennis court; for children, a play area with swings and slides; and for those who just want to relax, lovely rose gardens surrounding this historic castle.

~

Nearby Yuste monastery (10 km); Trujillo, Cáceres, Avila, within driving dista
Location at top of town, on a rock with gardens around it; with car parking
Meals breakfast, lunch, dinner
Prices rooms ⓔⓔⓔ; breakfast ⓔ; dinner ⓔⓔ
Rooms 43 double, 10 single, all with bath; all rooms have central heating, air-conditioning, phone, TV, minibar
Facilities 2 dining-rooms, 3 sitting-rooms, bar; swimming-pool, tennis court
Credit cards AE, DC, MC, V
Children welcome
Disabled ground-floor rooms
Pets not accepted **Closed** never
Manager Miguel Fages

CACERES

TRUJILLO

MESON LA CADENA
~ TOWN HOUSE ~

Plaza Mayor 5, 10200, Trujillo, Cáceres
TEL (927) 321463 **FAX** (927) 323116

A smaller, cheaper alternative to the Trujillo Parador is the Mesón La Cadena, on the main square. Situated in a rambling 16thC palace, it is really a restaurant (and noisy bar) with rooms, rather than a hotel, but it merits inclusion because of its central location and views over the square – a great place for watching the world go by from tables set out on the cobbled street.

The bedrooms are all on the third floor of this attractive granite house, far enough away from the noisy bar to be assured of a good night's sleep. They are simple and charming, with dark wooden furniture and brightly coloured rugs, woven locally. Rooms at the back have sloping ceilings, and look out on to the hill leading up to the castle.

One floor below is the restaurant, on three sides of a tiny internal courtyard, decorated with wrought iron lamps and local pottery plates on white walls. It is a lively place in the evenings, offering an interesting daily menu at a very reasonable price. The food is simple and good, and the waiters are friendly. The bar on the ground floor is also a popular spot and a good place to meet the locals.

~

Nearby Castle, palaces of the Conquistadors, old city walls. .
Location on main square in middle of town; car parking in square
Meals lunch, dinner
Prices rooms €€; meals €-€€
Rooms 8 double, all with bath; all rooms have central heating, air-conditioning, TV
Facilities dining-room sitting-room, bar
Credit cards AE, MC, V
Children welcome
Disabled access difficult
Pets not accepted
Closed never
Manager Juan Vicente Mariscal

CACERES

TRUJILLO

PT DE TRUJILLO

~ CONVERTED CONVENT ~

Plaza de Santa Clara, 10200, Trujillo, Cáceres
TEL (927) 321350

Built in 1984 in the 16thC convent of Santa Clara, this is one of the newest and one of the loveliest of Spain's Paradores. The setting is perfect – it is away from Trujillo's busy main square, in a maze of quiet, narrow streets overlooking the plains of Extremadura, yet within a walk of all the sights.

Some of the rooms are set in the old part of the convent, around a pretty courtyard full of orange and lemon trees. The cloisters lead off to a magnificent arched refectory through an ancient wooden door. This is now used as a bar and sitting area – a somewhat austere setting for writing postcards. The public rooms have been decorated with the convent in mind – furniture is simple, paintings are religious, and wooden crosses hang over the arches in the cloisters.

Half the bedrooms are in the nuns' old quarters, reached through low arched doorways from the gallery around the courtyard. The rest are in an adjoining modern building around a second courtyard. 'Lovely place, well furnished rooms', writes an American reader, who also noted that he found the staff 'a bit distant'.

~

Nearby castle, palaces of the Conquistadors, churches, old city walls and gates; Cáceres (50 km); Guadalupe (80 km).
Location on hill in narrow streets just outside town centre; with car parking and garage
Meals breakfast, lunch, dinner
Prices rooms ⓔⓔⓔ-ⓔⓔⓔⓔ; breakfast P
Rooms 45 double, one family room, all with bath; all rooms have central heating, air-conditioning, phone, TV, minibar, hairdrier
Facilities 2 dining-rooms, 2 sitting-rooms with TV
Credit cards AE, DC, MC, V
Children accepted **Disabled** ground-floor rooms
Pets not accepted **Closed** never **Manager** Secundino Fuertes Alvarez

BADAJOZ

MÉRIDA

HOTEL EMPERATRIZ

~ TOWN MANSION HOTEL ~

Plaza de España 19, 06800, Mérida, Badajoz
TEL (924) 313111 **FAX** (924) 313305
E-MAIL comercial@hotel-emperatriz.com **WEBSITE** www.hotel-emperatriz.com

Mérida is a lively historic town, although now (thanks to Moorish plundering of its stone) no more than half the size that it was in Roman times. The Emperatriz stands at its heart – a 16thC mansion, built of sandy-coloured granite in a privileged position on the main square.

The rather unprepossessing entrance opens into a grand cloistered courtyard, surrounded by granite pillars and arches on two floors. When we visited, dining-tables were laid in the courtyard for a wedding banquet – the effect was spectacular. The usual place to dine is an arched room off the cloisters, divided in two by elaborate wrought iron grilles. There are also two public bars, both underground, one serving tapas.

The hotel does not have all the facilities you expect in a Parador, but it has the character and sense of history that many of them lack. The bedrooms are all irregular shapes but are similarly furnished – embroidered bedspreads, wooden furniture and large bathrooms. Those with little balconies, facing on to the busy square full of outdoor cafés and ice-cream stalls, are rather noisy, at least by day.

~

Nearby Roman theatre, arena and villa, Alcazaba; Badajoz (60 km), Zafra (65 km), Cáceres (70 km), Trujillo (90 km).
Location on main square (follow signs to town centre); no private car parking
Meals breakfast, lunch, dinner
Prices rooms €€; breakfast €; meals €€
Rooms 17 double, 24 single, one family room, all with bath; all rooms have central heating, phone
Facilities dining-room, TV room, 2 bars
Credit cards V
Children welcome **Disabled** no special facilities **Pets** welcome
Closed never
Manager Francisco Moro

BADAJOZ

MÉRIDA

PT VIA DE LA PLATA
~ HISTORIC BUILDING ~

Plaza de la Constitución 3, 06800, Mérida, Badajoz
Tel (924) 313800 **Fax** (924) 319208

Mérida's chequered history is reflected in almost every room of the Parador Vía de la Plata (named after the Roman road it was built on). Roman friezes, acanthus capitals and ceramic urns come from the Augustan temple and Praetorian palace that stood here in Roman times. Visigothic stones and columns are evidence of a governor's residence, while Arabic inscriptions and decorations reveal later Moorish occupation. In the 16th century the Military Order of Santiago rebuilt the ruins as a monastery and their chapel now makes a stunning lounge. Although much of the Parador is modern, it is difficult not to get caught up in its intriguing web of history.

It stands on a quiet shady square, a short walk from the heart of town. Reception opens on to a pretty, typically Andalucian courtyard and a passage-way leads through to Moorish gardens. Most bedrooms look over the gardens, and are pleasant and spacious, with large marble bathrooms. Endless corridors lead to public rooms – a high-ceilinged sitting-room contrasting with a low beamed bar. All were busy when our inspectors visited, especially the dining-room, serving mouth-watering meals.

~

Nearby Roman theatre, arena and villa, Alcazaba; Badajoz (60 km), Zafra (65 km), Cáceres (70 km), Trujillo (90 km).
Location on quiet grassy square, in middle of old town; with garden and car parking
Meals breakfast, lunch, dinner
Prices rooms €€€€; breakfast €; meals €€€
Rooms 79 double, one single, 2 family rooms; all rooms have central heating, air-conditioning, phone, TV, minibar, radio
Facilities 3 dining-rooms, 5 sitting-rooms, 2 bars; swimming-pool, sauna, gymnasium
Credit cards AE, DC, MC, V **Children** welcome **Disabled** lift/elevator
Pets not accepted **Closed** never
Manager Victor Teodosio

BADAJOZ

ZAFRA

HOTEL HUERTA HONDA

∼ TOWN HOTEL ∼

Av López Asme 30, 06300, Zafra, Badajoz
TEL (924) 554100 **FAX** (924) 552504

When our inspectors first visited Zafra, the castle Parador was surrounded by scaffolding and in the throes of extensive redecoration. So they were delighted to discover, right next door, the Huerta Honda. This white villa, with red-tiled roofs and window-boxes dripping with geraniums, has fine views of the medieval castle. It is not merely a decent substitute for the Parador; in many ways, it is more attractive.

The hotel is built around a swimming-pool – the bedrooms on three sides, the dining-room on the fourth. Chairs and tables spill out of the bar and sitting-room around the pool, and it is a perfect place to enjoy a drink, between potted plants and trailing ivy. If you have had too much sun, you will appreciate the cool sitting-room, full of wicker furniture and wonderful ornaments (look out for the wicker pig under the mini grand piano, and the boar's head over the open fire). The dining-room is a similar haven, and the menu del dia excellent value. The hotel bar is a popular night spot and positively buzzes with activity. In contrast the bedrooms are serene; decorated in pastel shades with every possible comfort. You can be sure of a good night's sleep and of waking to a great view.

∼

Nearby Llerena (40 km), Aracena (90 km).
Location next to castle Parador in heart of town; with car parking
Meals breakfast, lunch, dinner
Prices rooms €€-€€€€; breakfast €; meals €€
Rooms 37 double, 29 with bath, 8 with shower; 9 single with shower; one family room with bath; all have central heating, air- conditioning, phone, TV, minibar, radio, hairdrier
Facilities dining-room, 2 sitting-rooms, 3 bars, terrace; swimming-pool
Credit cards AE, DC, MC, V
Children accepted **Disabled** access easy; ground- floor rooms; lift/elevator
Pets accepted **Closed** never
Manager María Encaruación Esteban

SEGOVIA

SEGOVIA

LAS SIRENAS
~ CITY HOTEL ~

Juan Bravo 30, 40001, Segovia
TEL (921) 462663 **FAX** (921) 462657

Built in the 1950s as Segovia's 'grand hotel', Las Sirenas has never quite made it to the top but fails gloriously in the attempt. (You will still find most of the interior glass doors ostentatiously etched 'GHLS' – Grand Hotel Las Sirenas.) The whole place is attractively faded and tarnished, and full of life, making Segovia's might-have-been far more appealing than many of the city's more modern and expensive lodgings, though a recent visitor found the atmosphere rather impersonal and unwelcoming.

You will probably spend most of your time paddling down long corridors, finding out where everything is. The building, with its long, wide entrance hall dotted with armchairs, pot plants and the odd grandfather clock, and its ceremonial staircase with padded handrail, includes a smoke-filled gentleman's club (or 'casino'), a cinema and a barber's shop. The sitting-room has a pleasant terrace bordered by wooden banisters: a quiet corner for breakfast. The bedrooms, simple and functional – often with parquet floors, polished mahogany furniture, substantial beds and new bathrooms – recall scenes from 1950s films. They are comfortable but not luxurious, and have a poor choice of lighting. Most are double glazed to keep out both the cold and noise.

~

Nearby Alcázar and aqueduct; La Granja (10 km).
Location on square of same name, in front of church of San Martin; with car parking
Meals breakfast
Prices rooms €€€; breakfast €
Rooms 24 double, all with bath; 9 single, 6 with bath, 3 with shower; 3 suites, 3 family rooms, all with bath; all rooms have central heating, air-conditioning, phone
Facilities sitting-room, bar, games room, terrace
Credit cards AE, DC, MC, V
Children welcome **Disabled** access easy; lift/elevator **Pets** not accepted
Closed never **Manager** Jesus Escudero

Segovia

Collado Hermoso

El Molino de Río Viejo

~ Converted mill ~

Carretera N110, km 172, 40170, Collado Hermoso, Segovia
Tel (921) 403063 **Fax** (921) 403051

This old mill set amongst poplars by the River Viejo makes a perfect base from which to explore the leafy countryside of Segovia. Horses are available to riding enthusiasts.

The bedrooms, some with beamed attic ceilings, are all the more cosy for the absence of mini-bar and TV. The dining-room is in the old mill room. From Monday to Thursday only pre-requested cold meals are served, but at the weekends you can try the chef's roast lamb and home-made strawberry tart.

Booking is essential. At weekends the hotel is very popular. At other times it may be closed if there are no reservations.

~

Nearby Sotosalbos (1 km); Pedraza (12 km); Segovia (18 km).
Location beside a main road; garden and car parking
Meals breakfast, lunch, dinner
Prices rooms €€; full board €€€; breakfast €
Rooms 6 double, all with bath; all rooms have central heating
Facilities sitting-room, bar, dining-room; satellite TV, library
Credit cards MC, V
Children welcome **Disabled** access difficult
Pets accepted **Closed** never **Proprietor** Coloma Armero

PARADORES IN CENTRAL SPAIN

The THREE PROVINCES to the north-west of Madrid have a handful of interesting Paradores. The 71-room one at Tordesillas is a low modern building set in a secluded pine-grove, just out of the town; it makes a good base for exploring this very interesting region of castles and medieval towns (Tel (983) 770051). Within easy reach of it is the PT de Segovia – modern, 106 rooms, on the edge of a lake, fine views of the town and cathedral (Tel (921) 443737). Near Avila is the 15thC PT Raimundo de Borgoña (see page 112) and, in the Sierra de Gredos, the rustic PT de Gredos near Navarredonda de Gredos, with its beamed ceilings and mounted hunting trophies (Tel (920) 348048).

With one exception, the Paradores to the north-east of Madrid (Soria and Sigüenza) and to the south (Chinchon, Toledo, Almagro, Alarcón) are all described in detail in this section. The exception is the unremarkable PT de Manzanares, east of Ciudad Real, which is a large white modern building in shady grounds (Tel (926) 613600).

SEGOVIA

PEDRAZA DE LA SIERRA

LA POSADA DE DON MARIANO

~ VILLAGE HOTEL ~

Calle Mayor 14, 40172, Pedraza de la Sierra, Segovia
TEL (921) 509886 **FAX** (921) 509887

If it is a quiet night, the manager of this archetypal charming small hotel, may offer you a selection of rooms. The trouble is: which one do you choose if all of them are like showpieces from an antiquated Ideal Home Exhibition?

Each is unique, personal, luxuriously carpeted and decorated with English floral wallpaper. Antiques abound. Everything is carefully arranged and prepared so that you could almost forget you are in a hotel. It comes as no surprise to learn that the hotel was designed by the owner of one of Madrid's most famous furnishing shops and was featured in *Elle* magazine. But that does not help you choose your room. Maybe you should just take your chance. How about one of the attic rooms upstairs? Smaller perhaps, but still exquisitely furnished and oozing with character. TVs are only provided on request – otherwise they spoil the decoration.

We had three minor reservations about the hotel: the noise from the bar below seems to travel to the rooms above it; the bathrooms are inadequately lit; and breakfast is disappointing. Otherwise, this is a hotel to remember.

~

Nearby Castle and square (2 mins walk each); scenic road up to Puerto de Navafría in the Sierra de Guadarrama (30 km).
Location near castle in main street; no private car parking
Meals breakfast, lunch, dinner
Prices rooms €€-€€€; breakfast €; meals *à la carte*
Rooms 15 double, 3 single, all with bath; all rooms have central heating, phone, TV (on request)
Facilities dining-room, sitting-room/bar
Credit cards AE, DC, MC, V
Children welcome **Disabled** access difficult **Pets** not accepted
Closed never
Manager Mariano Pascual

SORIA

SORIA

PT ANTONIO MACHADO
~ MODERN PARADOR ~

Parque del Castillo s/n, 42005, Soria
TEL (975) 240800 **FAX** (975) 240803

Prettily located, hanging off the side of a very green hilltop park, this modern brick-built Parador could be seen as a short guide to modern Spanish literature. It is named after the poet who lived and wrote in Soria but died in exile; you will find his blown-up image and his more famous poems on many of the pinkish walls.

Unlike most other modern Paradors, this one has not been contrived to look old. The furniture is as recent as the building and is occasionally brash and uncomfortable – but it may come as something of a relief after the rustic Castilian style of so many other Paradors. And if the hotel is short on charm, it has the compensating virtue of small size.

The entrance and reception are half-way up the building. There are bedrooms on the two floors above it and on one below. The higher up you go, of course, the better the view: 12 of the higher rooms offer vistas of Soria and the surrounding woodland; the rest are too low to see much from, or else look directly on to the quiet one-way road around the park outside. The dining- room and sitting-room are open-plan, separated by a wooden screen and sharing the same high, sloping ceiling; noise, unfortunately, travels easily between them.

~

Nearby San Juan de Duero monastery (1.5 km).
Location on hill overlooking city and Duero river; with car parking
Meals breakfast, lunch, dinner
Prices rooms ⓔⓔⓔ-ⓔⓔⓔⓔ; breakfast ⓔ; meals ⓔⓔ
Rooms 28 double, 4 single, 2 suites, all with bath; all rooms have central heating, phone, TV, minibar
Facilities dining-room, 2 sitting-rooms, bar
Credit cards AE, DC, MC, V
Children welcome **Disabled** access impossible
Pets not accepted **Closed** never
Manager Emilio Lafuente

AVILA

ÁVILA

GRAN HOTEL PALACIO VALDERRABANOS

~ CITY HOTEL ~

Plaza Catedral 9, 05001, Ávila
TEL (920) 211023 **FAX** (920) 251691

From its grand 15thC stone doorway, surmounted by an aristocratic family crest, to a room with a private tower, this spacious and calm hotel is pervaded by its past. Over reception you will find a graceful stone arch and old painted beams. In the hall, a glass case crammed full of antiques and curios for sale makes souvenir hunting easy.

The older, cosier rooms have floral wallpaper and beech furniture, but they occasionally feel uncomfortably half-empty. The thick shutters – which cut out noise – also shut out the daylight (the modern rooms on the third floor are much lighter). Some of the rooms have views across the square to the magnificent door of Ávila cathedral. But the real treat among them is room 229, from which a staircase ascends to a secluded sitting-room in the former watch-tower.

The slightly rustic white-walled restaurant in the basement (more attractive than the marbled dining-room upstairs) could be a museum of cookery – its intriguing exhibits including gigantic wine pots, an old sausage press (medieval, we were assured) and a vintage cheese churn.

~

Nearby Cathedral (opposite hotel), city walls (5 mins walk), St Thomas' Monastery (short drive); Guisando stone bulls (70 km).
Location next to cathedral in middle of town; no private car parking
Meals breakfast, lunch, dinner
Prices rooms ©©©-©©©©; breakfast ©; meals ©©
Rooms 62 double, 8 single, 3 suites, all with bath; all rooms have central heating, air-conditioning, phone, TV, minibar, radio, hairdrier
Facilities 2 dining-rooms, 3 sitting-rooms, bar
Credit cards AE, DC, MC, V
Children welcome **Disabled** access easy; lift/elevator
Pets accepted
Closed never
Manager Tomás Beltrán

AVILA

ÁVILA

PT RAIMUNDO DE BORGOÑA
~ CITY PARADOR ~

Marqués de Canales y Chozas 2, 05001, Ávila
TEL (920) 211340 **FAX** (920) 226166

In a corner of the old town, nestling against the city walls, this Parador is a careful mixture of old and new. Only the distinctive tower, and the shady courtyard with its tall pine tree, are left of the original 16thC building.

The rooms, like the building, divide into the old and the new. Those in the tower are somewhat cramped, with squeaky wooden floors. Those in the modern wings are larger, lighter and have better views. Some have four-poster beds. In others, the bed-frames look as if they had been made from sawn-up portcullises. In spring, birdwatchers should ask for room 209, from which there is a good view of storks nesting on an old belltower between March and June.

There are not many inviting places to sit indoors, but there is a sunny terrace outside the bar, and the courtyard is always fresh and cool. From the hotel it is only a short stroll to Ávila's famous city walls.

The restaurant serves a special dessert: soft, sweet balls named after Ávila's famous daughter – 'Saint Teresa's Yolks'.

~

Nearby Polentinos Palace and cathedral (5 mins walk); St Thomas' Monastery (a short drive); Guisando stone bulls (70 km); Sierra de Gredos (80 km).
Location near old walls in middle of city; small car park
Meals breakfast, lunch, dinner
Prices rooms ⓔⓔⓔ-ⓔⓔⓔⓔ; breakfast ⓔ; meals ⓔⓔ
Rooms 61 double, all with bath; all rooms have central heating, phone, TV, minibar, hairdrier
Facilities dining-room, sitting-room, bar, patio
Credit cards AE, DC, MC, V
Children welcome
Disabled access difficult; lift/elevator to 5 rooms
Pets not accepted
Closed never
Manager Juan de la Torre Alcalá

MADRID

Hotels in Madrid

Hotels in the city of Madrid cannot be conveniently divided into districts; they spread throughout the central area. The heart of the city is bounded by the Palacio Real and the railway terminus of the Estación del Norte on the west, and the wonderful Prado museum and gardens of El Retiro on the east, with the plaza of the Puerta del Sol roughly in the middle.

The Arosa (Tel (91) 532 1600) is a stylish building on the Gran Via, close to the Puerta del Sol. The rooms are elaborately decorated and well soundproofed to minimise noise from the busy street below. Also close to the Puerta del Sol is the Reina Victoria (Tel (91) 531 4500), an old favourite, with 195 reasonably priced rooms. The best of these overlook the pretty little plaza of Santa Ana.

Madrid is not blessed with the little gem-like hotels that are such a feature of Paris, Venice or Florence, for example. Real quality tends to go hand in hand with size and grandeur (and expense). For a once-in-a-blue-moon treat, there is the Ritz (Tel (91) 521 2857), which has been beautifully restored to reflect its former early-19thC glory. Public rooms are decorated with priceless carpets and tapestries, bedrooms are filled with antiques, service is absolutely immaculate; this is one of Spain's top hotels, a fact reflected in its prices. Nearby is the equally grand but rather less wonderful Palace (Tel (91) 360 8080), a massive 440-room hotel with an impressive clientele – from matadors to politicians. Service tends to be (not surprisingly) rather impersonal, but like the Ritz it has an excellent location close to the Prado. In contrast, the Villa Magna (Tel (91) 587 1234) is further from the middle towards the northern district. It is a modern version of the Ritz, and almost as classy. Set in immaculate gardens, it has a glass and steel tower, public rooms decorated in 18thC style, large bedrooms and stylish dining-rooms.

Outside the central area, there are two hotels worth mentioning. The Monte Real (Tel (91) 316 2140) is a modern hotel in an exclusive suburb. Ask for one of the rooms that overlooks the pool surrounded by trees in tranquil gardens. The hotel is far more impressive from the inside than from the outside; walls are hung with fabulous works of art and tapestries. The Barajas (Tel (91) 747 7700) is 14 km from the middle of the city, near the airport – ideal for anyone with an early flight. It has excellent facilities, including a swimming-pool, gymnasium, golf course and gardens.

Paying by credit card
We say in our factboxes which credit cards are accepted. Whether you do or do not value the free credit gained when paying by card, there are other advantages, particularly when making a payment in advance. Provided the card is a genuine credit card which permits you to borrow money for an extended period (Visa, Mastercard) and not a charge card which lacks that facility (American Express, Diners Club), paying with the card makes the credit card company jointly liable for fulfilment of your contract with the hotel. If you are not given the kind of room you wanted, for example, you can pursue a claim against the credit company when you get home.

MADRID

MADRID

HOTEL CARLOS V
~ CITY HOTEL ~

Maestro Vitoria 5, 28013, Madrid
TEL (91) 531 4100 **FAX** (91) 531 3761
E-MAIL recepcion@hotel.carlosv.com. **WEBSITE** www.hotelcarlosv.com.

At first sight this looks like a run-of-the-mill city-centre hotel and indeed the bedrooms, though renovated and spotless, and well-equipped with bright modern bathrooms, are impersonal. Scratch the surface, however, and you will find a family-run hotel that cares for its individual guests. The original owner's grandson, now in charge, eschews organised tour groups.

The hotel has a great variety of bedrooms including ones that interconnect and family rooms. Some rooms on the first and second floors have small balconies and five rooms at the top of the building have fair-sized, sun-catching terraces for no extra charge. The Carlos V is also one of the few hotels in its class in Madrid to have plenty of double beds. The hotel's greatest asset is its stylish sitting-room with its crystal chandeliers, large mirrors and moulded ceiling.

In a pedestrianized street next to the Puerta del Sol ('the centre of Spain'), the Carlos V can be a maddening place to find in a car. The convenient location has its disadvantages. A good night's sleep in summer depends on getting the right balance between ventilation, street noise and the din of the air-conditioning.

~

Nearby Metro (Callao or Sol, 2 mins walk), Plaza Mayor.
Location on a pedestrianized street near Puerta del Sol; public car parking nearby
Meals breakfast
Prices rooms €€€€; break-fast €
Rooms 61 double, 6 single, all with bath; all rooms have central heating, air-conditioning, phone, satellite TV, minibar, hairdrier, safe
Facilities sitting-room, bar/breakfast room
Credit cards AE, DC, MC, V
Children welcome **Disabled** access easy; lift/elevator **Pets** not accepted
Closed never
Proprietor Nicolás Gutierrez

MADRID

MADRID

HOTEL SERRANO
~ CITY HOTEL ~

Marqués de Villamejor 8, 28006, Madrid
TEL (91) 5769626 **FAX** (91) 5753307

On a side street off Madrid's prestigious, modern north-south axis, the Paseo de la Castellana (the place to be seen these days), the Serrano is a small hotel for anyone in search of a little non-central exclusivity.

The building – unashamedly modern, with a grimy façade – is well designed inside, with plenty of light and space. Moreover, it has been conscientiously decorated and furnished, often with reproduction period chairs and tables. There are also a few genuinely antique objects. The large, sombre 18thC tapestry on the wall of the sitting-room-cum-bar is, we were assured, a priceless national treasure.

In a Spanish city hotel with so few rooms, you can expect some extras – such as special massage showers in all bathrooms. The three suites are moderately luxurious; their sitting-rooms alone are bigger than many entire hotel rooms. There are even magazines on the coffee tables – a personal touch for a chain hotel.

Warts and all, here you get the feeling that you are one of a very few select guests and can make yourself a little at home. A modest alternative to the Ritz at a fraction of the price.

~

Nearby Metro (Rubén Darío station, 5 mins walk); the Prado and Retiro Park (2 km); Plaza Mayor and old city centre (3 km).
Location in a quiet street near Paseo de la Castellana; no private car parking
Meals breakfast
Prices rooms €€€-€€€€; breakfast €
Rooms 24 double, 5 single, one family room, 4 suites, all with bath; all rooms have central heating, air-conditioning, phone, TV, minibar, hairdrier, safe
Facilities sitting-room/bar
Credit cards AE, DC, MC, V
Children welcome **Disabled** access difficult; lift/elevator **Pets** not accepted
Closed never
Manager Laura Gil

MADRID

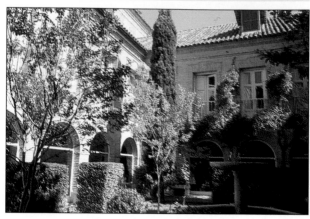

PT DE CHINCHON
~ CONVERTED MONASTERY ~

Avenida Generalisimo 1, 28370, Chinchón, Madrid
TEL (91) 894 0836 **FAX** (91) 894 0908
E-MAIL chinchon@parador.es

Gathered around a light, green, airy courtyard – with tall cypress trees in its corners and pigeons flitting around a fountain and climbing roses – the ground floor of this 17thC monastery is a wealth of colour and detail. The peaceful, glazed-in cloisters form wide passages which are decorated with murals and antiques: clocks, chests, cabinets, even a large old brass still (the town is renowned for its *anis*).

The stately dining-room and cool blue bar are both brightly tiled and lit by small windows piercing massively thick walls. Climb the staircase, which has original but fading frescoes on the ceiling above it, and you find landings furnished with comfortable sofas.

The bedrooms are different in style from everything else. They have the austere but romantic atmosphere of a decaying medieval palace; but very clean, light, airy and comfortable. Our most recent reporter noticed the thoughtful and friendly service and thought the food good, even though the menu was somewhat unenterprising. Fair prices, too.

~

Nearby Plaza Mayor; Royal Palace, Aranjuez (26 km).
Location opposite main square in heart of village; private garage
Meals breakfast, lunch, dinner
Prices rooms ⓔⓔⓔⓔ; breakfast ⓔ meals ⓔⓔ
Rooms 38 double, all with bath; all rooms have central heating, air-conditioning, phone, TV, minibar, hairdrier
Facilities 2 dining-rooms, sitting-room, bar, terrace
Credit cards AE ,DC ,MC, V
Children welcome
Disabled access not easy; some ground-floor rooms
Pets not accepted
Closed never
Manager José Menguiano

MADRID

EL PAULAR

HOTEL SANTA MARIA DEL PAULAR
~ CONVERTED CLOISTER ~

28741, El Paular, Rascafría Madrid
TEL (91) 869 1011 **FAX** (91) 869 1006
E-MAIL reservas@paular.palace-hotel-madrid.es

You don't often get the chance to stay in a four-star hotel next to – and sharing its premises with – a Benedictine monastery. The Santa María occupies the old cloisters, entered by means of a monumental arch.

Sadly, the chain that runs this hotel is more interested in its up-market facility-rich image than in artistic heritage. The mock-historical style of decoration scarcely does justice to the handsome surroundings. You will just have to use your imagination. But it is a peaceful place, surrounded by trees and with plenty of space to stretch out – a popular location for conferences and wedding receptions. There is also a choice of places to eat. Apart from the dining-room, a *méson* offers lamb cooked in the traditional way, in a wood-fired oven.

The bedrooms are simple, sober and Castilian in style – which in this part of the world tends to mean that they have characterless woodwork and wrought iron light fittings. You might prefer to call them austere or spartan: more suitable for a monastic retreat, and certainly less than you would expect from this class of hotel. Most have views of either the courtyard or the garden, and the grand mountains beyond.

~

Nearby Monastery church (next door).
Location in mountains of Sierra de Guadarrama, near village; with garden and car parking
Meals breakfast, lunch, dinner
Prices rooms €€-€€€€; breakfast €€; meals €€
Rooms 36 double, all with bath; 17 single, 2 with bath, 15 with shower; 5 suites, all with bath; all rooms have central heating, phone, TV
Facilities 2 dining-rooms, sitting-room, bar, games room; swimming-pool, tennis courts, mountain bikes
Credit cards AE, DC, V
Children welcome; under 12s free; special play area **Disabled** access difficult
Pets accepted if small **Closed** never **Manager** Manuel Iruela

GUADALAJARA

SIGÜENZA

PT CASTILLO DE SIGÜENZA

~ CASTLE PARADOR ~

Plaza del Castillo, 19250, Sigüenza, Guadalajara
TEL (949) 390100 **FAX** (949) 391364
E-MAIL siguenza@parador.es

Other castles seem small in comparison with this massive example, which stands defiantly alone on a hill above the town that it guards, at the top of a steep cobbled street.

Unfortunately, the most interesting bits – the towers and battlements – are out of bounds. But there is plenty left to explore. Near Room 239, for example, an inconspicuous slit in the wall leads to a secret balcony high over the silent 13thC Romanesque chapel.

The sitting-room ('the throne room'), held up by six stone pillars and containing two fireplaces, is big enough for giants to repose in, and is sprinkled with regal chairs crowned with gold knobs. The layout is rather formal, in contrast to the inviting stone-arched bar, with its benches and leather chairs.

The bedrooms come with or without overhanging wooden balconies overlooking the large courtyard, with its ornamental hedges and soothingly gurgling fountain, but one balcony (Room 210) dangles daringly over the castle's outer walls. Twelve rooms now have four-poster beds. The walls between rooms are not all of fortress proportions; we found that the noise of other guests' televisions, plumbing and conversations travelled easily.

~

Nearby Roman arch at Medinacelli (20 km), Atienza (30 km).
Location on hill overlooking town, at top of steep cobbled street; with car park
Meals breakfast, lunch, dinner
Prices rooms €€€-€€€€, breakfast €; meals €€
Rooms 76 double, 3 single, 2 family rooms, all with bath; all rooms have central heating, air-conditioning, phone, TV, minibar
Facilities dining-room, sitting-room, bar, patio; gymnasium
Credit cards AE, DC, MC, V
Children welcome **Disabled** access easy; lift/elevator **Pets** not accepted
Closed never **Manager** Juan Carlos Sánchez

TOLEDO

TOLEDO

LA ALMAZARA

~ COUNTRY HOUSE HOTEL ~

Ctra Toledo-Arges km 3.4, 45080, Toledo
TEL (925) 223866 FAX (925) 250562
WEBSITE www.frontpage-98.com/hotelalmazara/home.htm

Just a few kilometres out of Toledo is this hotel on a wooded hilltop over-looking the city. The views are magnificent –and cost half the price of the Parador further around the hill. It is a simple, rustic place, built as a country residence in the 16thC. A gravel courtyard is surrounded on three sides by a solid ivy-clad building.

This is not the sort of place you would want to lounge around in all day, and it does not have a restaurant, but it is the perfect haven after a hot day's sightseeing in much-visited Toledo. 'Absolute peace' writes a contented American visitor. 'The place is charming, the staff are charming, even the cats are charming.' The atmosphere is very laid back.

The huge sitting-room looks lived in – comfy sofas around a log fire, piles of magazines and books scattered on tables, and a TV in one corner. Breakfast is served in a delightful arched room that leads on to a small (and rather overgrown) terrace. All the bedrooms are simple, cool and spacious (extra beds can be installed), and are brightened up by locally-made curtains and bedspreads. Bedrooms 1 to 9 all have balconies over-looking Toledo.

~

Nearby Toledo – Alcázar, cathedral, El Greco museum, synagogue and Jewish quarter; Madrid (70 km).
Location on hill overlooking Toledo; 3 km from Carretera Circunvalación, on Cuerva road; with car parking in courtyard. Well signposted.
Meals breakfast
Prices rooms €-€€€; breakfast €
Rooms 22 double, 2 single, one family room, all with bath; all rooms have central heating, phone
Facilities sitting-room, breakfast room
Credit cards AE, DC, MC, V
Children welcome **Disabled** 6 ground-floor rooms **Pets** not accepted
Closed 10 Dec to 1 Mar **Manager** Paulino Villamor

TOLEDO

TOLEDO

HOSTAL DEL CARDENAL
∼ COUNTRY HOTEL ∼

Paseo de Recaredo 24, 45004, Toledo
TEL (925) 224900 **FAX** (925) 222991
E-MAIL cardenal@macom.es

This classy little hotel was one of the highlights of our last inspection tour. It occupies a long, pale-brick mansion, built in the 18thC as the summer residence of the archbishop of Toledo, Cardinal Lorenzana. It is set in beautiful shaded gardens, virtually enclosed by the old city walls, rising in three tiers to an impressive, crested doorway. The lowest tier of the garden incorporates an excellent restaurant, now run independently but used by all the guests.

Every room oozes style and character; the sitting-rooms contain well-chosen antiques, the stairway has a beautiful sculpted ceiling, bedrooms have old painted-wood bedheads, and bathrooms have hand-painted tiles and old mirrors. There is a clever mixture of old and new throughout; original Moorish corbels support beams in the upstairs corridor, while modern Moorish sculpture surrounds bedroom doors downstairs. There are two brick courtyards, decorated with ferns, terracotta pots and lilies.

This is a magical place to enjoy a warm summer's evening. You need to book well in advance as it is extremely popular, especially with British and American tourists.

∼

Nearby Alcázar, cathedral, El Greco Museum, synagogue and Jewish quarter; Madrid (70 km).
Location within city walls near main gate (Puerta de Bisagra); with garden but no private car parking
Meals breakfast; lunch and dinner in adjacent restaurant of same name
Prices rooms €€-€€€€; breakfast €; dinner in restaurant €€
Rooms 22 double, 3 single, 2 suites, all with bath; all rooms have central heating, phone; most have air-conditioning, hairdrier, TV
Facilities breakfast room, 2 sitting-rooms
Credit cards AE, DC, MC, V
Children welcome **Disabled** no special facilities
Pets accepted **Closed** never **Proprietor** Luis González

TOLEDO

TOLEDO

PINTOR EL GRECO
~ TOWN HOTEL ~

Alamillos del Tránsito, 13, 45002 Toledo
TEL (925) 214250 **FAX** (925) 215819
E-MAIL elgreco@estanciases.es **WEBSITE** pintorelgrecosl@airtel.net

You could hardly be closer to the sights of Toledo than in this converted and extended 17th century house in the former Jewish quarter of the city.

Behind the original façade, most of the building is modern but the widespread use of sand-blasted pine, wrought iron and Spanish ceramics preserves the historical feel while allowing light, space and all modern comforts.

You can get a feel of the original building by taking the short flight of steps beside Room 3 (which has a brick arch in its bathroom) down to the entrance of a blocked tunnel which once linked the house to the palace behind, and indeed to the city at large.

Some of the bedrooms overlook the square and gardens in front of the hotel and two of the rooms have views of the hillside across the river. There are six secluded rooms in the attic, two of them large family rooms.

If all the hotel lacks is a dining-room, there are plenty of restaurants close by and the owners have their own beyond the city walls.

Prices increase for Toledo's Holy Week celebrations.

~

Nearby El Greco museum, El Tránsito synagogue, cathedral.
Location next to El Greco museum; no car parking
Meals breakfast
Prices rooms €€; breakfast €
Rooms 33 double, one single, all with bath; all rooms have central heating, air-conditioning, TV, minibar, telephone, safe, hairdrier
Facilities sitting-room, breakfast room
Credit cards AE, DC, MC, V
Children accepted
Disabled ramp available, lift to 2nd floor **Pets** accepted
Closed never
Manager Mariano Sánchez

CUENCA

HOTEL LA CUEVA DEL FRAILE
~ COUNTRY HOTEL ~

Carretera de Buenache, Hoz del río Húecar, 16001, Cuenca
TEL (969) 211571 **FAX** (969) 256047

Set in the same green, high-walled valley as the city of Cuenca, this is a larger hotel than at first it appears to be, and the 16thC ancestry to which it lays claim is scarcely in evidence, for all its blackened beams. But the hotel, gathered around a brilliant-white courtyard, does have many other virtues.

There is a great variety of public rooms on the ground floor taking in numerous seating areas and a rather gloomy bar with comfortable settees. There is also a good choice of activities, including a pool and tennis court, and bicycles for hire. The hotel has a children's play area. The bedrooms are divided into the old, the new and the very new. In almost all of them the 'old' wooden beams of the ceiling clash with the new white wood of the doors and cupboards. If you want something special, room 130 is a tasteful suite with a cottage-style sitting-room and rocking chairs.

The hotel makes an excellent base for excursions to Cuenca and its scenic surroundings. Ask Fernando on reception for the best places to go: he is the co-author of one of the best guide books to the area.

~

Nearby Cuenca; Ventano del Diablo (30 km); Ciudad Encantada (45 km).
Location in gorge of river Húecar, 7 km from Cuenca on Buenache road; with garden and car parking
Meals breakfast, lunch, dinner
Prices rooms €€€-€€€€; breakfast €; meals €€
Rooms 56 double, 4 single, one suite, 2 family rooms, all with bath; all have central heating, phone, hairdrier, TV
Facilities 3 dining-rooms, 4 sitting-rooms, bar, billiards, dance floor; swimming-pool, tennis court
Credit cards AE, DC, MC, V
Children welcome; play area; baby-sitting
Disabled access possible; 8 ground-floor rooms **Pets** not accepted
Closed Jan and Feb **Proprietor** Francisco de Borja García

CUENCA

CUENCA

POSADA DE SAN JOSÉ
~ TOWN HOUSE HOTEL ~

Calle Julian Romero 4, 16001, Cuenca
TEL (969) 211300 **FAX** (969) 230365
E-MAIL psanjose@arrakis.es

Once the home of the in-laws of Velazquez's daughter and later a cathedral choir school, this Posada could hardly offer better credentials. Today – with a 1961 addition – it is a six-tier labyrinth replete with curios, antique furniture and even frescoes. If you like stairs, antiques, history and exploring, this is the hotel for you.

Jennifer Morter, an expatriate Canadian, and her Spanish husband Antonio have lovingly decorated every room with great attention to detail and cleanliness ('you could sit on the floor', Jennifer likes to say). The sheets are pressed and turned back in the old-fashioned way. The 30 rooms are all different and each has been given individual character – you may get a four-poster bed, a Latin inscription on the wall or a dreamy balcony with a magnificent view across the valley. Room 33 is the most popular, with its sloping floor and two balconies.

The rooms themselves are cosy enough to sit in but there is also a rambling breakfast room and bar where tapas is served, with intimate nooks and a sunny terrace, a TV room stranded on its own peculiar floor and a hall with a few antiques and a sofa.

~

Nearby Cathedral and Casas Colgadas (both within a short walk); Ventano del Diablo (25 km), Ciudad Encantada (35 km).
Location off Plaza Mayor in old part of town, down narrow road past cathedral; no private car parking
Meals breakfast, light snack suppers
Prices rooms €-€€€; breakfast €; meals €€
Rooms 21 double, 16 with bath; 5 single, 2 with bath; 1 triple; 4 family rooms with bath; all rooms have central heating
Facilities breakfast room, TV room, bar
Credit cards AE,DC, V
Children welcome **Disabled** access difficult **Pets** accepted in bedrooms
Closed never; bar only, Mon **Proprietors** Jennifer Morter and Antonio Cortinas

CUENCA

ALARCON

PT MARQUÉS DE VILLENA

~ CASTLE PARADOR ~

Avenida Amigos del Castillo, 16213, Alarcón, Cuenca
TEL (969) 331350 FAX (969) 330303
E-MAIL alarcon@parador.es

You may not believe your eyes as you approach Alarcón, so improbable is the position of the castle which has guarded the village since Moorish times – overlooking the valley of the deep-green Río Júcar, on the edge of Don Quixote's La Mancha.

You may feel like a wandering knight returning from the Crusades as you step into the quaint little courtyard with its well in the middle. Within the thick castle walls you should sleep well and live in typical Parador style, with your minibar discreetly hidden in a reproduction antique cabinet; the pick of the bedrooms is number 103, with a canopied bed and steps up to a high window where distressed damsels might sit and dream of rescue. The sitting-room-cum-cafeteria has everything you could want of a great hall: a circular iron chandelier, an enormous tapestry depicting a coat of arms, a suit of armour and three wooden thrones. The dining-room is also a vaulted chamber, with a long slit window.

A lift will whisk you up to the battlements for a view worthy of a feudal baron. The village has several other historical buildings and there are some good walks.

~

Nearby Castle of Belmonte (70 km), Mota del Cuervo (85 km) and Cuenca (85 km).
Location on huge rock encircled by river, at end of village; car parking outside castle
Meals breakfast, lunch, dinner
Prices rooms €€€€; breakfast €; meals €€
Rooms 12 double, one single, all with bath; all rooms have central heating, phone, TV, minibar
Facilities dining-room, sitting-room, bar
Credit cards AE, DC, MC, V
Children welcome; special play area **Disabled** access difficult; lift/elevator
Pets not accepted **Closed** never **Manager** Aurora Lozano

CUENCA

MOTA DEL CUERVO

MESON DE DON QUIJOTE

~ TOWN HOTEL ~

Francisco Costi 2, 16630, Mota del Cuervo, Cuenca
TEL (967) 180200 FAX (967) 180711

If Don Quixote himself was not to be taken too seriously, then neither is his *mesón*, which is inauspiciously located behind a petrol station in a little town overlooked by windmills in the heart of La Mancha.

The whole ground floor – with its cartwheel chandeliers, theatrical staircase, papier-maché well and cobbled inn-courtyard-cum-lounge (where the ingenious hidalgo could easily have been knighted) – flirts with the memory of Cervantes' hero. All that is lacking is the buxom Dulcinea. Fixtures and fittings are typically 'rustic' and Castilian – history as it never was. The chunky dining-room chairs, all nuts and bolts, must have been a fascinating woodwork project for somebody. The bar-stools are reminiscent of something out of a medieval torture chamber.

The waiters are dressed in 'traditional' costume, with broad red cummerbunds, grey waistcoats and bootlace ties. The restaurant's excellent menu includes a hearty vegetarian bean soup and home-made rice pudding. Unfortunately, the rustic illusion stops short of the bedrooms, which are fairly nondescript. But the rest of the hotel should keep you well entertained. 'Great fun, very friendly, very Spanish', writes a contented reader.

~

Nearby Belmonte Castle (15 km); El Toboso (15 km).
Location behind filling station on main road through town; with car parking
Meals breakfast, lunch, dinner
Prices rooms €€; breakfast €; meals €€
Rooms 28 double, 7 single, one suite, all with bath; all rooms have central heating, air-conditioning, phone
Facilities dining-room, 3 sitting-rooms, bar; swimming-pool
Credit cards AE, DC, MC, V
Children accepted **Disabled** access difficult **Pets** not accepted
Closed never
Proprietor José María Palacios

CIUDAD REAL

ALMAGRO

PT DE ALMAGRO

~ CONVERTED CONVENT PARADOR ~

Ronda de San Francisco, 13270, Almagro, Ciudad Real
TEL (926) 860100 **FAX** (926) 860150

Almagro's Parador has ancient origins (it is on the site of a 16thC Franciscan convent) but is almost entirely modern, built just a decade ago. The layout of the building is highly unusual – the rooms are set around fourteen little quads, all different from each other. The first one you come to has ivy-clad walls and fig trees shading a small fountain, the second bamboo trees around a pond, the third rose-bushes, and so on.

It would be easy to get lost inside – every corridor looks the same – if it were not for the lovely hand-painted signs and room numbers on every corner. Such attention to detail runs throughout – there are painted ceilings and bright tapestries in the public rooms, tiled bed-heads and locally made lace covers in the bedrooms, and fresh flowers throughout. The *bodega* is built on two floors in the old cellars of the convent; massive storage jars go up through the floor and are used as table tops on the upper level. Other cosy sitting-rooms are dotted about.

Despite its size, this is one of the friendliest Paradors – an interesting place in a picturesque town on the plains of Don Quixote's La Mancha.

~

Nearby Plaza Mayor, old town, lace-making; Ciudad Real (25 km); Valdepeñas (35 km).
Location in quiet street, near centre of town, signed from main road; with garden and car parking
Meals breakfast, lunch, dinner
Prices rooms €€-€€€€; breakfast €; meals €€
Rooms 48 double, 6 single, one suite; all with bath; all rooms have central heating, air-conditioning, phone, TV, minibar
Facilities 2 dining-rooms, 2 sitting-rooms, bar, terrace; swimming-pool
Credit cards AE, DC, MC, V
Children welcome **Disabled** access easy **Pets** not accepted **Closed** never
Manager José Maria Lopez de Santos

Teruel

VALDEROBBRES

Torre del Visco

~ CONVERTED TOWER HOUSE ~

Apartado 15, 44580 Valderrobres, Teruel
TEL (978) 769015 **FAX** (978) 769016

This is a remote 15thC semi-fortified estate house which has been carefully restored by its English owners, Piers and Jemma Markham, who have lived in Spain for many years. It's a real hideaway: the nearest villages are 7½ miles (12 km) away, and the hotel is reached by gravelled forest tracks. Arriving at the final turn in the track, you see at last the outline of the house, surrounded by 200 acres of farmland. Standing on a steep hillside overlooking the beautiful valley of the river Tastavins, it is a haven of peace, with a warm welcome from the owners. You can walk, ride or mountain bike along the valley or up into the mountains, followed by rest and relaxation on the terrace, in the sitting-room with its grand piano and open fire, or in the library. Breakfast is taken in the farmhouse kitchen, while dinner features Mediterranean cuisine using produce from the farm as well as fish bought directly from the quayside. The bedrooms are fresh, with modern paintings on the walls and tiled floors, and the whole place feels like a home, not a hotel. A reader writes in exceptionally fulsome terms about the place, emphasizing the value for money. Evening meal obligatory.

~

Nearby Valderrobres, 7.5 miles (12 km); Morella, 33 miles (53 km).
Location 7.5 miles (12 km) S of Valderrobres; hotel signposted after 3.5 miles (6 km); in own farmland with ample parking
Meals breakfast, lunch, dinner
Prices rooms €€€€ (including breakfast and dinner); lunch €€€
Rooms 11 double, 3 suites, all with bath; all rooms have central heating, hairdrier
Facilities 4 sitting rooms, dining room, library, bodega, terrace, gardens
Credit cards MC, V
Children accepted **Disabled** access difficult
Pets not accepted
Closed Jan 8-19
Proprietors Piers and Jemma Markham

TERUEL

MIRAMBEL

FONDA GUIMERA
~ HISTORIC VILLAGE INN ~

Calle Agustín Pastor 28, 44141, Mirambel, Teruel
TEL (964) 178269 **FAX** (964) 178293

Take a walled medieval village – complete with watch-tower, numerous Gothic palaces and wide cobbled streets – restore all these elements carefully, and what you have is Mirambel, once acclaimed the 'most beautiful village in Spain' by Queen Sofía.

The old *fonda* has also been restored. Its façade on the main street is in keeping with the rest of this historic village but everything behind it is ultra-new. All the bedrooms are modern and comfortable. Although half provide nothing more than basic accommodation, those at the back of the building have small bathrooms and balconies, and the central heating is needed in winter.

The Fonda is a simple, inexpensive place to stay and it does not have a sitting-room or any other public facilities. But you can always have a drink with the locals in the small, gloomy public bar next door which doubles as reception (don't be put off by its appearance), and with a restaurant behind.

The village itself is a fascinating place to stroll around and is set in magnificent countryside, reminiscent of the Yorkshire Dales, which is good for walking and cycling. It is still just off the beaten tourist track, and worth the detour.

~

Nearby Cantavieja (15 km), Morella (30 km).
Location on cobbled street in village; no private car parking
Meals breakfast, lunch, dinner
Prices rooms €; breakfast € ; meals €
Rooms 18 double, 8 with bath; some rooms have central heating
Facilities dining-room, bar
Credit cards V **Children** welcome **Disabled** access difficult **Pets** not accepted
Closed never
Manager Pedro Guimerá

TERUEL

ALCAÑIZ

PT LA CONCORDIA
~ CASTLE PARADOR ~

Castillo de los Calatravos, 44600, Alcañiz, Teruel
TEL (978) 830400 **FAX** (978) 830366

Still dominating the town and its green river from the summit of a hill, as it has done since the 12th century, this castle-monastery is the first thing that you see as you approach Alcañiz; it certainly looks too big to have only 12 rooms.

Although monumental in scale, the former home of the Order of the Knights of Calatrava has been converted into an intimate hotel full of historical character. It is furnished in a modern imitation of castle-style, with wrought iron chandeliers everywhere and gold knobs topping the chairs in a dining-room fit for medieval banquets. In the bedrooms, however, you can forget that you are in a castle, as evidence of the past has been largely crowded out by new furnishings. There are magnificent views from most of the rooms and the rest look on to the peaceful cloister-garden behind.

The castle is also a tourist attraction and its grounds are open to the public – so it is not a place in which to seek seclusion. The TV in the cafeteria at the entrance, in an elegant vaulted chamber, sometimes intrudes too, but at night the castle returns more or less to its ancestral peace.

~

Nearby Caspe (30 km) – Roman temple, caves of Molinos (40 km), El Parrisal near Beceite (50 km) – wildlife.
Location on hill dominating town (follow Parador signs); with garden and car parking
Meals breakfast, lunch, dinner
Prices rooms €€€€; breakfast €; meals €€
Rooms 10 double, 2 single, all with bath; all rooms have central heating, air-conditioning, phone, TV, minibar
Facilities 2 dining-rooms, 2 sitting-rooms, cafeteria
Credit cards AE, DC, MC, V
Children welcome **Disabled** access easy; lift/ elevator **Pets** not accepted
Closed 18 Dec to 1 Feb
Manager Miguel Cruz

CASTELLON

MORELLA

HOTEL CARDENAL RAM

~ CONVERTED PALACE ~

Cuesta Suñer 1, 12300, Morella, Castellón
TEL (964) 173085 FAX (964) 173218

Cardinal Ram's 16thC Gothic palace, set in a commanding position on Morella's medieval porticoed main street, is a local landmark. Its thick walls enclose a variety of spacious rooms. The furnishings have been improved since we last visited. Bathrooms are modern and well-equipped, and the rooms on the second and third floors have magnificent views.

The excellent restaurant is well known for its local delicacies including the succulent *cordero trufado* – lamb stuffed with truffles – the hearty Morella soup, and typical desserts made of sheep milk, *cuajada* and *requesón*. We are glad to report that breakfast is much improved.

The hotel lacks seating and recreational space, but it makes up for this with its age and character. It is arguably overpriced for the level of comfort offered, but you can eat well here and it is as close to the authentic history of Morella as you will get.

~

Nearby Castle and church; La Balma (25 km), Montalvana –cave paintings (25 km), Mirambel (30 km) – walled village.
Location in heart of Morella, on main street; private car parking
Meals breakfast, lunch, dinner
Prices rooms €€-€€€€; breakfast €; dinner €€
Rooms 16 double, 1 single, 2 suites, all with bath; all rooms have central heating, phone, TV, minibar
Facilities dining-room, hall/sitting-room
Credit cards MC, V
Children accepted
Disabled access difficult
Pets not accepted
Closed never
Proprietor Peñarroya Fabregat

VALENCIA

Hotels in Valencia

Valencia, Spain's third largest city, is relatively little-visited by tourists. Its international fame rests mainly on paella. In Spain it is also known for its nightlife (facilitated by year-round balmy temperatures), its prolific production of oranges and the spectacular Fallas fiesta in March during which huge papier mâché monuments are burnt in the streets. It is the capital of a large region on the eastern seaboard, including numerous cultural tourist attractions still undiscovered by the hordes.

Most of the city's hotels cater predominantly for trade fair and business visitors. The best are a long way out of town. The purpose-built seaside Parador, Luis Vives (Tel (96) 161 1186), is on the edge of a nature reserve and surrounded by a golf course. Nearby is another modern hotel, the Sidi Saler Palace (Tel (96) 161 0411). The luxurious 82-room Monte Picayo (Tel (96) 142 0100), the choice of VIPs, is a short way inland, (conveniently close to the A7 motorway) and has its own casino and adjacent bullring.

In the city centre, apart from the Excelsior (see below), the best of the smaller hotels is probably Hotel Inglés (Tel (96) 351 6426), housed in an old palace. The art nouveau-style Reina Victoria (Tel (96) 352 0487), with 94 rooms, retains an air of the belle époque in which it was built. A much larger central hotel is the modern Astoria Palace (Tel (96) 352 6737).

Hotel Excelsior

~ City hotel ~

Calle Barcelonina 5, 46002, Valencia
Tel (96) 3514612 **Fax** (96) 3523478

Handsome, old and mostly refurbished, the Excelsior offers greater comfort and charm than many of Valencia's more expensive hotels. Despite the odd plastic plant, the whole place is imbued with past elegance: the stairs are carpeted, the lift has brass doors and old furniture is scattered here and there. Many of the bedrooms are let down by their small bathrooms with old fittings, but the suites, with their brass bedsteads, painted cornices, floral textiles and cosy ante-rooms, are highly desirable. Away from your room, you have to choose between a noisy bar and a somewhat formal English-style sitting-room.

~

Nearby Palacio del Marqués de Dos Aguas, Lonja, market.
Location in middle of town, near Plaza del Ayuntamiento; no private car parking
Meals breakfast, lunch, dinner
Prices rooms ©©-©©©©; breakfast ©; lunch ©©, dinner ©
Rooms 38 double, 18 single, 9 family rooms, all with bath; all rooms have central heating, air-conditioning, phone; most rooms have TV
Facilities dining-room, sitting-room, cafeteria
Credit cards AE, DC, MC, V
Children welcome **Disabled** easy access; lift/ elevator
Pets not accepted **Closed** never **Manager** Anna Ivanes

VALENCIA

XATIVA

HOSTERIA DE MONT SANT

~ COUNTRY HOTEL ~

Subida al Castillo, s/n, Xativa, Valencia
TEL (96) 227 5081 **FAX** (96) 228 1905

A delightful little ochre-red country house, well restored, set in lovely grounds, with great views down on to Xativa and above to the Moorish castle: with just six bedrooms, this is essentially a charming restaurant with rooms. The welcome is warm, the atmosphere relaxed; the service is faultless and every detail has been thought out - all in a way that a larger place could not imitate. It is recommended by two widely-travelled readers, who were impressed by the friendly atmosphere, spotless maintenance, efficient organization, large beds and all-round comfort.

There's a spacious sitting-room with French windows making the most of the views; an intimate dining-room with doors to a terrace for eating outside. The menu is 'excellent' and reasonably priced. Bedrooms, all decorated indivually, are simply furnished in Spanish period style. The Castle Room has particularly good views. It would be worth pausing here for more than just one night in order to explore historic Xativa, and to mellow out beside the secluded swimming-pool.

~

Nearby Xativa, Valencia, Alicante.
Location near the castle; in own large gardens, with car parking, signposted
Meals breakfast, lunch, dinner
Prices €€€€
Rooms 6, four double, two suites, all with air-conditioning, central heating
Facilities sitting-room, dining-room, terrace, swimming- pool.
Credit cards AE, MC, V
Children welcome
Disabled 1 room suitable
Pets accepted
Closed never
Proprietor Javier Andreas Cifre

ALICANTE

CALPE

VENTA LA CHATA

~ ROADSIDE INN ~

Carretera Nacional 332 km 172, 03710, Calpe, Alicante
TEL & FAX (96) 583 0308

It is easy to imagine coaches drawing up at this old inn a hundred years ago to change horses and set down passengers for the night. Since then it has been restored and partly modernized, keeping the old flavour but adding some of the comforts that modern travellers expect.

The rooms are varied, mixing old and new furniture in a piecemeal assortment. Most of the bathrooms have ageing fittings. Ask for a room with a terrace-suntrap overlooking the leafy, peaceful garden. Some of the rooms also have views of Calpe's Gibraltar-like rock, the Peñón de Ifach.

Downstairs there are informal tables in the breakfast/TV room in front of reception and more inviting chairs and tables on the two terraces and under the arches of the entrance porch. The cool, open-plan sitting-room, decorated with old pots, gourds and an enormous gold-framed mirror, has some cosy armchairs. The restaurant, popular with non-residents, is lit by a long line of windows and has a door leading into the garden. Among the cactuses, clumps of bamboo and flowers that gather around a mature carob tree, there are some quiet, shady corners.

~

Nearby Calpe (5 km), Peñón de Ifach (10km), Altea (15 km), Jávea (25 km), Castell de Guadalest (35 km).
Location on main N332 (Valencia to Alicante), 4 km north of Calpe; with garden and car parking
Meals breakfast
Prices rooms €-€€; breakfast €
Rooms 16 double, one single, all with bath; all rooms have TV, phone
Facilities dining-room, 2 sitting-rooms, terrace; tennis court
Credit cards AE, DC, V
Children welcome; play area in garden **Disabled** access difficult
Pets accepted
Closed never
Proprietor María Giner

ALICANTE

ROSA

~ BEACH HOTEL ~

Congre 3, Las Marinas, 03700, Denia, Alicante
TEL (96) 5781573 **FAX** (96) 6424774

DENIA, WITH ITS BALMY Mediterranean climate, won the heart of Michel Kessous, Parisian by birth and globetrotter by inclination, who arrived on holiday at the beginning of the 1970s and still has not moved on. His hard work and optimism have brought about the conversion of the humble pension, which he built, into a handsome villa with colonnaded façade and Florentine-style balconies.

The bedrooms in the main house are somewhat narrow and have recently been redecorated and equipped in the manner of a grand hotel; the self-catering bungalows are more suitable for a holiday with children or for a long stay. Inviting swimming-pool, and a short step to the beach.

~

NEARBY Denia castle (1 km); Les Rotes beach (4 km).
LOCATION off the coast road; garden and car parking
MEALS breakfast, lunch, dinner **PRICES** rooms €€€-€€€€; breakfast €; meals €€€ **ROOMS** 34 double, 1 single, 5 small suites, all with bath; all rooms have central heating, air conditioning, phone, safe, satellite TV, hairdrier, iron
FACILITIES dining-room, bar, terrace; swimming-pool, tennis court, table tennis
CREDIT CARDS MC, V **CHILDREN** very welcome; playground and paddling pool
DISABLED access easy; some specially equipped rooms **PETS** small pets accepted
CLOSED Nov to Mar **PROPRIETOR** Michel Kessous

Swiss Hotel Moraira

~ Seaside resort hotel ~

Urbanización Club Moraira, 03724, Moraira, Alicante
Tel (96) 5747104 **Fax** (96) 5747074

THE Swiss watches on sale in the lobby and the private hair salon set the tone for this hotel which goes for luxury at the expense of personality.

Set in an estate of holiday villas a short way back from the coast, its central feature is the large swimming-pool surrounded by a sun-trapping terrace onto which all rooms have views and more or less direct access. The bedrooms are spacious, especially the 'semi-suites' and suites, and lavishly equipped – all newly furnished, although in predictable grand hotel style. The staff are discreet and faultlessly formal. Only breakfast is served.

~

Nearby Peñón de Ifach (12km); Jávea (14km); Jalón Valley.
Location 1.5km from Moraira (signposted off Calpe road) **Meals** breakfast
Prices rooms €€€€-€€€€€; breakfast €
Rooms 18 double, 5 semi-suites, 2 suites, all with bath; all rooms have central heating, air-conditioning, TV, minibar, telephone
Facilities sitting-room, bar, swimming-pool
Credit cards AE, DC, MC, V
Children accepted **Disabled** easy access **Pets** accepted at extra charge
Closed never **Manager** Santiago Bravo

ALICANTE

CASTELL DE CASTELLS

PENSION CASTELLS

~ VILLAGE GUEST HOUSE ~

Calle San Vicente 18, 03793, Castell de Castells, Alicante
TEL & FAX (96) 5518254
E-MAIL castells@darburn.com **WEBSITE** www.darburn.com

Having converted an old village house and found themselves with a sur-
plus of rooms, previous owners Jan and Eric Wright decided to put
them to profitable use. New owners Martin and Camilla Darburn, also
English, are continuing to run things along the same lines.

From the street you step directly into the sitting-cum-dining- room. At
the window end, by the street door, is the table around which everyone
eats together. At the other end comfy armchairs are arranged by the
hearth. Upstairs are four simple but cosy rooms, each a different shape; all
of them furnished with a loving touch. Two of them have sloping beamed
roofs. The top one, dubbed 'the Casita', is the favourite: by the bed are a
shelf of books and a tea-maker. The staircase ends in a sunny terrace at
rooftop level.

Although Castell de Castells is not far from the Costa Blanca it gets few
tourists and the principal attraction is rural peace. Many of their guests
come to walk in the surrounding mountains, guided by Martin, although
potential visitors are warned that there is little for children to do in the
area. If you don't mind sharing your table with whoever else happens to be
staying, this is one definition of the charming small hotel.

~

Nearby natural rock arches (5km); Jalon valley vineyards (20km); Castell de
Guadalest (33km); Costa Blanca (35km).
Location in a narrow street in the centre of the village: park near the church and
ask for directions.
Meals breakfast, dinner
Prices rooms €€; Continental breakfast €, English breakfast €; dinner €€
Rooms 3 twin, one double, all with shower and toilet; all rooms have central
heating
Facilities sitting/dining-room; guided walks (Pts 2000 per person)
Credit cards none **Children** accepted **Disabled** access difficult
Pets not accepted **Closed** Jul and Aug **Proprietors** Martin and Camilla Darburn

MURCIA

ARCHENA

Hotel Termas

~ Spa hotel ~

Balneario de Archena, 30600, Archena, Murcia
Tel (968) 670100 **Fax** (968) 671002
E-mail reservas@balneario_archena_sa.es **Website** www.balneario_archena_sa.es

The oldest and most attractive of the three hotels in a leafy spa founded by the Romans, the Termas is decorated inside in a superb Mozarabic style. With its cupolas, patios and ornate plasterwork, at times you could believe that you were staying in the Alhambra. Most guests come for the waters, and there is a rest-cure calm in the sitting-room with its coffered ceiling and card tables. The bedrooms are pleasantly modern, some of them looking through eucalyptus trees to the river. Two floors down is a labyrinth of humid tunnels heated by warm water which gushes out of the ground.

~

Nearby Murcia (25 km); Alcantarilla waterwheel (30 km).
Location by river Segura, through town (follow signs); with grounds and car parking **Meals** breakfast, lunch, dinner
Prices rooms €€-€€€€; breakfast€; meals €€
Rooms 60 double, 10 single, all with bath; all have central heating, air-conditioning, phone, TV, minibar, radio
Facilities dining-room, sitting-room; spa; swimming-pool, 2 tennis courts
Credit cards accepted **Children** welcome **Disabled** easy access; lift/ elevator
Pets not accepted **Closed** never **Manager** Mercedes Coghen

---

PARADORES IN EASTERN SPAIN

THE PARADORES ON the east coast of Spain are modern and function-al, with little charm. The PT Costa del Azahar at Benicarlo is a box-like building (108 rooms) set in beautiful gardens facing 6 km of gently curving beach (Tel (964) 470100). Just south of Valencia, on the narrow sandy peninsula of El Saler is the PT Luis Vives, a golf hotel with its own 18-hole course (Tel (96) 161 1186). Further down the coast on the Javea peninsula is another unremarkable 1960s cre-ation, the 65-room PT Costa Blanca (Tel (96) 5790200). The PT de Puerto Lumbreras, 80 km SW of Murcia, is not on the coast, despite its maritime-sounding name. It is a plain but smart white hotel (60 rooms) on the main road through the town. Its floors are chequered marble, and the walls are brightened up by local ceramics (Tel (96) 8402025)

Of the places further inland, only the PT La Concordia at Alcañiz (a hilltop castle with just 12 rooms) gets a full entry here (see page 129). The PT de Teruel is a modern hotel overlooking the city which is famous for its integration of Christian, Jewish and Muslim styles of architecture (Tel (978) 601800). The PT de la Mancha, south of Albacete, is a low, white building on the sprawling plains of La Mancha. It is decorated in rustic style with beamed ceilings and primitive wooden farm tools hanging from the walls – donkey bas-kets, oxen yokes, ploughshares (Tel (967) 229450).

HUELVA

LOS MARINES

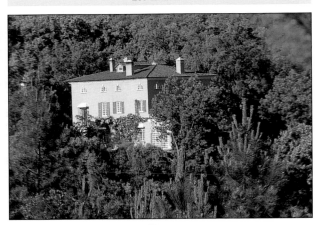

FINCA BUENVINO
~ COUNTRY HOTEL ~

21293, Los Marines, Huelva
TEL (959) 124034 **FAX** (959) 501029
E-MAIL buenvino@facilnet.es **WEBSITE** www.buenvino.com

As our inspectors discovered, this is not an easy place to find; the lovely modern villa, built in 18thC style on the top of a hill, is hidden away in the heart of a National Park, amid chestnut forests, fruit trees and bubbling springs.

Sam and Jeannie Chesterton, an English couple, stress that this is their home and that you are expected to join in with the family (who are very easy-going). They keep Iberian pigs, sheep, goats and chickens, and have three dogs. Everyone eats together – on the terrace in summer or in the panelled dining room. Jeannie is a trained cordon bleu cook, and produces mouth-watering dinners and salad lunches, accompanied by liberal amounts of wine. Drinks taken at other times – and perhaps consumed before the huge fireplace of the sitting-room or in the airy conservatory – are recorded in an 'honesty book'.

The bedrooms are all bright and comfortable. The two attic rooms have hand-stencilled walls and wonderful views over the woods. The other two rooms are smaller; one has its own bathroom and dressing-room, the other requires a trip across the landing. There is also a self-catering cottage with its own small plunge pool, for those seeking greater seclusion.

~

Nearby Aracena (caves and castle); Zafra (85 km).
Location in heart of woodland, km 95 of N433 Seville-Lisbon road, W of Los Marines, itself W of Aracena; with garden and shaded car parking
Meals breakfast, light lunch (on request), dinner
Prices DB&B €€€
Rooms 4 double, two with bath; all rooms have central heating, hairdrier, kettle
Facilities dining-room, sitting-room, TV room, conservatory; swimming-pool
Credit cards MC, V
Children welcome **Disabled** access difficult **Pets** not accepted
Closed Aug; Christmas and New Year (check by phone before visiting)
Proprietors Sam and Jeannie Chesterton

HUELVA

ARACENA

SIERRA DE ARACENA

~ TOWN HOTEL ~

Gran Via 21, 21200, Aracena, Huelva
TEL (959) 126175/126019 **FAX** (959) 126218

THE ATTRACTIVE TOWN of Aracena is built in tiers on a hillside crowned by the remains of a Templar castle. Beneath it, underground rivers have carved out vast narrow caves full of spectacular formations, coloured by iron oxide – well worth exploring if you are passing through the region.

The Sierra de Aracena, in the wide, cobbled Gran Vía, makes a good base for an overnight stay. It is a solid, square building with an elaborate brick-patterned façade and arches around the ground-floor windows. It is a quiet, sleepy hotel, where the world drifts by without intruding; a few locals may wander in to watch the TV. The sitting-room is pleasantly furnished with wicker chairs, floral fabrics and tiled pictures, and adjoins a modern bar (which doubles as a breakfast room). There is an open fire in winter.

The bedrooms are simple and comfortable. The ones at the back have great views of the castle and Aracena's winding streets and red-tiled roofs. They are all kept spotlessly clean by the friendly staff, who don't speak a word of English but seldom stop smiling. There is no dining-room but several recommended restaurants are to be found in the town. A recent inspector had poor first impressions, including lack of hot water and a smell in the bathroom, possibly of drains; balanced by a very friendly welcome.

~

NEARBY Cave of Marvels, castle; Zafra (95 km).
LOCATION on quiet wide street in middle of town; with parking for 3 cars
MEALS breakfast
PRICES rooms €-€€; breakfast €
ROOMS 30 double, 10 single, 2 suites, all with bath; all rooms have central heating, phone, radio, TV (in 12 double rooms), minibar
FACILITIES sitting-room, bar/breakfast area **CREDIT CARDS** AE, DC, V
CHILDREN accepted **DISABLED** lift/elevator; some ground-floor rooms
PETS not accepted **CLOSED** never **MANAGER** María del Carmen Fernández

SEVILLE

CARMONA

PT ALCAZAR DEL REY DON PEDRO

~ CASTLE PARADOR ~

41410, Carmona, Seville
TEL (95) 4141010 FAX (95) 4141712
E-MAIL carmona@parador.es

With 65 rooms and conference facilities, this Parador can hardly be described as 'small and charming'. But it merits inclusion because of its superb location on a hill top above the busy walled town of Carmona. The views are breath-taking.

The Moorish fortress that stood here was transformed into a luxury palace by the craftsmen of the Seville Alcázar for the infamous Don Pedro the Cruel. The Parador architects have taken great care to recreate the 'palace' atmosphere, setting elegant Mudejar columns around a pretty internal courtyard and decorating the stonework and floor tiles with the familiar Moorish star pattern. Extensive renovation was also carried out in 1997.

The public rooms are large and comfortable; glass cases of swords and armour and hanging tapestries give them a 'stately home' feel, but on our visit both the sitting-rooms and cavernous dining-room seemed positively animated. Top-floor bedrooms have amazing views over the fertile plains of the Corbones river. The rooms show more attention to detail than the average Parador room (we had great trouble locating the disguised minibar).

~

Nearby Roman remains; Seville (35 km), Ecija (55 km) – palaces and churches; Córdoba (105 km).
Location on top of hill in Carmona (follow Parador signs); with garden and ample shaded car parking
Meals breakfast, lunch, dinner
Prices rooms ©©©-©©©©, breakfast © meals ©©
Rooms 60 double, 3 single, all with bath; all rooms have central heating, air-conditioning, phone, TV, hairdrier, minibar, radio
Facilities dining-room, 2 sitting-rooms, bar; swimming-pool
Credit cards AE, DC, V
Children welcome **Disabled** most rooms are on ground floor **Pets** not accepted
Closed never **Manager** Benito Montañés

Seville

Casa de Carmona

~ Historic palace hotel ~

Plaza de Lasso, 1, 41410, Carmona, Sevilla
Tel (95) 4191000 **Fax** (95) 4190189 **E-mail** schwabach@casadecarmona.com

This hotel is housed in a 16thC palace in the heart of Carmona. Built in Andalucian style, with a distinct Mudejar influence, it has a two-storey, porticoed central patio and a delightful interior garden. The sitting-room, with its delicate starry ceiling and period pieces reflected in a large Napoleon III mirror, testifies to the fashion and fine art background of the owners, who have faithfully restored the building and filled it with treasures. The cosy bedrooms, are a touch more modern, with light flowery fabrics and all creature comforts alongside attractive antique furniture. A recent visitor, was very impressed, not least by the helpful reception staff.

~

Nearby old town and castle; Roman necropolis; Seville (30 km).
Location in one of the most important squares in the city; garden and car parking outside
Meals breakfast, lunch, dinner
Prices rooms €€€€; breakfast €€; meals €€
Rooms 13 double, 18 suites, all with bath; all rooms have air conditioning, telephone, radio, minibar, satellite TV
Facilities sitting-room, dining-room, bar; swimming-pool, mini-gym, sauna
Credit cards AE, DC, MC, V
Children accepted **Disabled** access easy **Pets** accepted
Closed never **Manager** Felipe Guardiola Medina

CATEGORIES AND STARS

Every hotel in Spain is categorised as either Parador, hotel, apartment hotel, *hostal*, motel or *pensión* and given a star rating. Although stars and categories sometimes provide a guide to price and facilities, they say little about the ambience and quality of service you can expect. Many charming hotels have only one or two stars and more than one four-star hotel has failed to impress our inspectors.

Some hotels in the book style themselves posada, venta, fonda, mesón etc. These names derive from older types of wayside lodging and are no longer official categories.

SEVILLE

SEVILLE

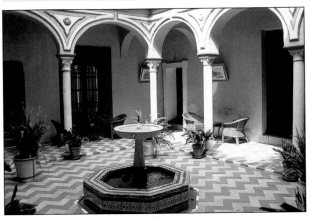

LAS CASAS DE LA JUDERIA

~ TOWN HOUSE HOTEL ~

Callejún de Dos Hermanas, 7, 41004, Seville
TEL (95) 4415150
FAX (95) 4422170

This is the largest and best known of the several Sevillan mansions to have been converted into stunning but affordable hotels during the 1990s. Book well in advance. The interconnected houses, dating from the 17thC, are most memorable for their beautiful mustard-and-green courtyards, awash with pot plants, urns and statuary. The cool main patio, where wicker chairs are set around a tiled fountain under marble pillared arcades, is a strong contender for the prettiest spot in the city.

Bedrooms, with parquet floors and prints of old Seville, are exceedingly tasteful. Many have sitting areas, and much more besides – a pillar here, old tilework there, maybe a mini, private patio (such as number 29). Generally, first-floor rooms are preferable, since they have french windows opening on to small balconies overlooking the courtyards.

The hotel's location – down a cul-de-sac alley in the Santa Cruz or Jewish quarter – is hard to beat: very quiet yet as central as can be. Though only breakfast (good buffets) is on offer, endless tapas bars lie a short walk away. The place is professionally run: for example, if you're having trouble finding the hotel by car, you can call a porter to pick up your vehicle and park it for you.

~

Nearby Cathedral, La Giralda, the Alcázar, Jewish quarter.
Location In the heart of the Santa Cruz district; underground car park
Meals breakfast
Prices rooms €€-€€€€; breakfast €
Rooms 46 double, 10 single, 31 suites, all with bath; all rooms have central heating, TV (satellite), phone, air-conditioning, minibar
Facilities breakfast room, bar
Credit cards AE, DC, M, V
Children welcome
Disabled lift/elevator, but limited access **Pets** No **Closed** never
Manager Miguel Cazorla Cuadro

SEVILLE

LAS CASAS DEL REY DE BAEZA
~ TOWN HOUSE HOTEL ~

Plaza Cristo de la Redenciûn, 2, 41004, Seville
TEL (95) 4561496 **FAX** (95) 4561441

This new hotel, which opened in 1998 under the same dynamic owner-ship as the Casas de la Juderìa (see page x), is a slick conversion of an 18thC apartment block. Depending on your taste, youíll either find it a stylish fusion of old architecture and modern design, or a mite contrived. It focusses around three whitewashed, cobbled patios. They are decorated with baskets of oranges and stone flour grinders, are candlelit at night, and surrounded by wooden galleries painted a washed blue. Bedrooms, most of which overlook the patios, are equally eye-catching. Colourful rugs cover black granite floors, armchairs come in plush leather, and bath-rooms in orange and grey marble. Lighter rooms have french windows and small balconies looking across the little square in front of the hotel to a former convent.

The hotel has limited facilities - beyond the bedrooms, there is just a small rooftop swimming pool and a breakfast room/bar. However, you can expect good buffet breakfasts with freshly-squeezed orange juice. The location, in a little-visited part of the Barrio Santa Cruz, has a lot going for it. The big sights are just a ten-minute walk away, while the nearby tapas bars are full of locals rather than tourists.

~

Nearby Casa de Pilatos, Jewish quarter, shopping district.
Location overlooking small square off narrow street; underground parking
Meals breakfast
Prices €€€-€€€€; breakfast €
Rooms 42 doubles, 2 suites, all with bath; all rooms have central heating, air-conditioning, TV (satellite), phone, minibar
Facilities breakfast room, bar, swimming pool
Credit cards AE, DC, M, V
Children accepted **Disabled** lift/elevator, but access difficult **Pets** No
Closed never
Manager Jose Alfonso Martinez Espejo

SEVILLE

SEVILLE

HOTEL DONA MARIA

~ TOWN HOUSE HOTEL ~

Don Remondo 19, 41004, Seville
TEL (95) 4224990 FAX (95) 4229546
E-MAIL reservas@hdmaria.com WEBSITE www.hdmaria.com

Imagine lying by a swimming-pool which overlooks one of the biggest cathedrals in the world – just one of the perks of staying at the Doña María in the heart of Seville. The hotel is built in an old town house, in a cobbled alley-way off the cathedral square – very convenient for sightseeing, not so convenient for parking, unless you get a space in the underground car park.

The hotel has no dining-room, but serves large buffet breakfasts downstairs, and has two bars – one wood-panelled, adjoining the sitting-room, the other on the roof-terrace (in summer only). The other public rooms are elegant and comfortable – the sitting-room has dark red sofas between brick pillars, the landings are crammed with antiques and portraits, the corridors are lit with blue and white glass lamps; and there is a tiny tropical garden in the middle of the building.

Each bedroom is different, apparently decorated by the Marchioness de San Joaquin herself and named after eminent Sevillian ladies. If possible, ask to see several rooms and choose carefully, as some are disappointing and not cheap. The roof-terrace certainly makes up for it – there are not many places where you get a view of Gothic spires as you swim.

Nearby Cathedral, La Giralda, the Alcázar, Jewish quarter.
Location in narrow alley-way, leading from square in front of cathedral; underground parking for 9 cars
Meals breakfast **Prices** rooms €€€-€€€€; breakfast €
Rooms 35 double, all with bath; 14 single, 12 with bath, 3 with shower; all rooms have central heating, phone, TV, radio; swimming-pool on roof
Facilities 2 sitting-rooms, bar, breakfast room
Credit cards AE, DC, MC, V
Children welcome
Disabled lift/elevator **Pets** accepted in 2 bedrooms
Closed never **Manager** Isabel Moreno

SEVILLE

SEVILLE

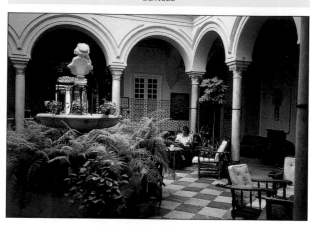

HOTEL SIMON

~ TOWN HOUSE HOTEL ~

García de Vinuesa 19, 41001, Seville
TEL (95) 4226660

Don't be put off by the neon sign outside; once inside the white wrought iron gates, you find yourself transported back in time. Behind them is the typical Andalucian courtyard of a beautiful Moorish town house – a perfect place to cool down among the ferns and marble busts after a busy morning's sightseeing in this spectacular city.

Decoration in the hotel is reminiscent of a mosque; the walls are covered in pretty Moorish tiles and gilded mirrors. Glass chandeliers hang down between the slender marble pillars. The stairway and corridors have tiled walls and floors, period furniture and cabinets full of silver. Bedrooms tend to vary in size and quality and are the original rooms of this lovely 18thC house. Some have small balconies looking on to the street, while others are rather small and airless. Bathrooms also vary, but all are spotlessly clean.

The staff are friendly and helpful, and obviously take great pride in this unusual hotel. The Simon has only two disadvantages – it can be noisy inside and there's no car parking immediately outside. But it is possible to park nearby and the hotel could not be more central.

~

Nearby Cathedral, La Giralda, the Alcázar, Jewish quarter.
Location on small street, just west of cathedral; no private car parking
Meals breakfast
Prices rooms €€-€€€; breakfast €
Rooms 19 double, 15 with bath, 4 with shower; 5 single with shower; 3 suites with bath; all rooms have central heating, phone, air-conditioning
Facilities dining-room, sitting-room, patio
Credit cards AE, DC, MC, V
Children accepted **Disabled** some ground-floor rooms
Pets accepted in bedrooms
Closed never
Manager Francisco Aguayo

SEVILLE

SEVILLE

HOTEL MURILLO
~ TOWN HOUSE HOTEL ~

Lope de Rueda 7 & 9, 41000, Seville
TEL (95) 421 6095 FAX (95) 421 9616
E-MAIL murillo@nexo.es WEBSITE www.sol.com/hotel-murillo

To find the Hotel Murillo you need a good sense of direction and a detailed map; it is lost in the historic Barrio de Santa Cruz, a maze of tiny pedestrian passages behind the Alcázar. From the outside, it is a typical Sevillian town house, painted mustard-yellow and white, with wrought-iron grilles and balconies.

From the inside, it is an extraordinary place, a treasure trove of peculiar objects and antiques. Suits of armour guard the entrance to a long, dim room crammed with furniture –leather sling chairs around carved tables, elaborate screens and glass cabinets along the walls, a sedan chair in front of the bar. The panelled ceiling gives you the feeling that you are in the cabin of a medieval ship. This room serves as a sitting, eating and reception area, and there is another small sitting-room for families or groups.

In contrast, the bedrooms upstairs are rather plain. Second-floor rooms have small balconies looking on to the street, third-floor rooms have arched windows. Furniture is functional and bathrooms small. The room keys are attached to miniature paint pallets, emphasizing the connection with the Sevillian artist Murillo, after whom the hotel is named.

~

Nearby Cathedral, La Giralda, the Alcázar, Jewish quarter.
Location in a maze of tiny streets, north of cathedral, approachable only by foot; garages nearby
Meals breakfast
Prices rooms €€-€€€; breakfast €
Rooms 47 double, all with bath; 10 single, with bath,; all rooms have central heating, air-conditioning, phone
Facilities sitting-room, bar
Credit cards AE, DC, MC, V
Children accepted **Disabled** lift/elevator **Pets** not accepted
Closed never **Manager** Enrique Ysasi

SEVILLE

PATIO DE LA CARTUJA/PATIO DE LA ALAMEDA

~ TOWN HOUSE APARTMENTS ~

CARTUJA: Lumbreras, 8-10, 41002, Seville. **TEL** (95) 4900200 **FAX** (95) 4902056.
ALAMEDA: Alameda de Hèrcules, 56, 41002, Seville.
TEL (95) 4904999 **FAX** (95) 4900226.

We've lumped these two apartment hotels together because they are under the same management, are just 150 yards apart, and offer virtually identical accommodation at the same (bargain) prices. The Cartuja is a rebuilt 19thC apartment block around a wedge-shaped courtyard (or patio), while the Alameda, set around three cool, ochre-coloured patios, was formerly a mansion, then a hospital. At both, almost all the apartments overlook the patios so are peaceful (avoid the few facing the busy roads). All are furnished in a cheerful modern style, and have a large sitting-room with a sofabed, plus kitchenette and compact bedroom. The area, albeit on the up, is slightly seedy: hence the low rates.

~

Nearby Macarena, Isla Magica, city centre 20-minute walk away.
Location on busy streets in the Macarena; underground garages
Meals breakfast
Prices apartments €€-€€€; breakfast €
Rooms 34 apartments at Cartuja, 22 at Alameda, all with bath; all have central heating, TV, phone, air-conditioning
Facilities breakfast room at Cartuja
Credit cards AE, DC, M, V
Children welcome
Disabled some ground floor rooms
Pets No
Closed never
Manager Fransisco Ramirez

SEVILLE

SEVILLE

SAN GIL
~ TOWN HOUSE HOTEL ~

Calle Parras, 29, 41002, Seville
TEL (95) 4906811
FAX (95) 4906939

Another Sevillan mansion turned hotel – this time dating from the early 20thC and located in the earthy Macarena district (take a taxi rather than walk around here late at night). Memorable features include the riot of colourful tiles covering the walls in the public areas, and large, tranquil courtyard garden, with olive trees, palms and an old cypress. You can also chill out by the small rooftop swimming pool.

Bedrooms are spread through the mansion, an old converted factory and new block, all of which surround the courtyard. They are simply decorated but notably light and spacious, with a sofabed and kitchenette, and some are split over two floors.

~

Nearby Macarena sights; city centre 20-minute walk away.
Location on Macarena backstreet; garage nearby
Meals breakfast
Prices rooms €€€-€€€€, including breakfast
Rooms 21 double, 18 suites, all with bath; all rooms have central heating, TV (satellite), phone, air-conditioning, minibar, safe
Facilities bar, breakfast room, swimming pool
Credit cards AE, DC, M, V
Children welcome
Disabled no special facilities
Pets no
Closed never
Manager Aquilino Fraile

SEVILLE

ALCALA DE GUADAIRA

HOTEL OROMANA
～ ANDALUCIAN VILLA ～

Avenida de Portugal, 41500, Alcalá de Guadaira, Seville
TEL & FAX (95) 5686400

Our inspector had trouble finding the Oromana; it is on a hill opposite the town, in an area (of the same name) which is rapidly being developed for residential purposes, eating into the pine woods that surround the hotel. The tranquillity is not yet lost; a long winding drive takes you away from the building sites to the rounded knoll where this impressive white hotel, complete with bell-tower, overlooks the meandering Guadaira river.

There is a particularly Spanish feel to the lofty public rooms; reception leads into a vaulted sitting-room of marble columns and ornamental Spanish vases. Its large French windows open on to a bougainvillaea-clad terrace where guests can sit and enjoy the view. Next door is a small cosy bar, serving *tapas* at red-and- white checked tables. The more formal dark green dining-room has sombre pictures of matadors on the walls. All service comes with a smile.

The bedrooms are in the main building and in a new extension which overlooks the swimming-pool. The rooms, decorated in light tones, vary in size but not quality. Some have balconies – a welcome extra in the heat of the Andalucian summer. A recent visitor was unenthusiastic about the food, and thought a worn stair carpet might be dangerous. Reports welcome.

～

Nearby Seville (15 km) – cathedral and palaces.
Location amid pine trees, on hill overlooking town and river; with gardens and ample car parking
Meals breakfast, lunch, dinner
Prices rooms €€-€€€€€; breakfast €; dinner €€
Rooms 26 doubles, one single, 3 family rooms; all with bath; all rooms have central heating, air-conditioning, phone, TV
Facilities dining-room, 2 sitting-rooms, bar/cafeteria, terrace; swimming-pool
Credit cards AE, DC, V **Children** welcome **Disabled** lift/elevator
Pets not accepted **Closed** never **Manager** Cristina Martinez

SEVILLE

AZNALCAZAR

HACIENDA DOS OLIVOS
~ COUNTRY GUEST HOTEL ~

Aznalcazar, Seville
TEL & FAX (95) 575 05 62
E-MAIL j.beattie@teleline.es

THE NAME REFERS to the only two olive trees which had to be cut down to build this typical estate house a decade or so ago. A mixture of Andalucían, Moorish and modern, it is surrounded by a sea of olive groves which are farmed by the owners. Within easy reach of Seville, the property borders the vast Doñana National Park.

Hacienda Dos Olivos is run very much as a private home. Meals are taken communaly, either in the candle-lit dining room, or, on fine evenings, beneath an olive tree in the gardens. The two guest bedrooms, grouped around an inner patio, are simply furnished, with tiled floors and high sloping beamed ceilings. It is possible to take the whole property for a single party, including La Casita, a little self-catering house within the courtyard which sleeps four.

The *raison d'être* of the Hacienda is its magnificent horses. Johanna Beattie-Batista is a renowned Classical dressage rider, and while staying here you can, if you wish, take lessons. We continue to get mixed reports about this place. 'A personal favourite' says a trusted inspector – 'simple, no frills; very Adalusian – you are part of the family'. 'Dirty, unusable swimming pool' says another visitor – 'generally in need of attention'. We suggest you avoid it if you want regular comforts and faultless housekeeping; if your priority is atmosphere and something different, it's great.

~

NEARBY Seville, 22 miles (35 km); Doñana National Park; Christopher Columbus sights on the Costa de la Luz.
LOCATION outside Aznalcazar, 22 miles (35 km) SW of Seville; in own grounds with ample parking. Difficult to find. Get directions from reception.
PRICES rooms €€-€€€; meals €€
ROOMS 5 double and twin, one with bath, 4 sharing 2 bathrooms; all rooms have heating
FACILITIES sitting room, dining room, courtyard, terraces, gardens, swimming pool
CREDIT CARDS not accepted **CHILDREN** welcome **DISABLED** rooms on ground floor
PETS not accepted **CLOSED** never **PROPRIETOR** Johanna Beattie-Batista

SEVILLE

CRUCE DE LAS CABEZAS

HACIENDA DE SAN RAFAEL

~ COUNTRY HOTEL ~

Apartado 28, Carretera Nacional IV (Km 594)
TEL (908) 632 748 **FAX** (908) 750 349
Bookings only through TRI Hotel Marketing, London, Tel 020 8563 2100 Fax 020 8563 2300

A discrimating London couple, not to mention one of our regular reporters, recommend this stunning place less than an hour south of Seville. One small negative is the inauspicious approach from the main-road, the NIV, and the setting in flat farmland. But once down the drive, the charm takes over: the two-storey building, formerly an olive farm and press, has impeccably white outside walls contrasting with windows and cornices picked out in tasteful cream-ochre: come the golden light of a fine evening, the whole place glows. A young Sloany girl may greet you on arrival; most of the guests are British.

Most of the rooms are set around the large, oblong, pleasingly paved interior courtyard, with the old well neatly restored at its centre. Public rooms offer exemplary Hispanic rustic chic. There's a pleasant atmosphere in the grand drawing room, where you help yourself to drinks. Dinner is a pricey set menu, but the French chef ensures that it's all delicious. The split-level bedrooms have simply-patterned rugs on tiled floors, and homely-but-smart patchwork quilts in artfully muted colours; 'galleries' give sitting areas under exposed beams. Breakfast is brought to one's private terrace. An exclusive experience.

It's a major outing to get anywhere – but you can always just relax by one of the two pristine pools.

~

Nearby Seville, Jerez, Arcos, Ronda
Location just off the NIV south of Seville, signposted; in own grounds with car parking. Directions given on booking.
Meals breakfast, lunch, dinner
Prices €€€
Rooms 11; 9 double, 2 twin; all with bathrooms
Facilities drawing-room, dining-room, garden, 2 swimming-pools, paddle tennis
Credit cards none. **Children** discouraged. **Disabled** one specially adapted room
Pets not accepted **Closed** 20 Nov-10 Mar **Proprietors** Tim and Kuky Reid

CORDOBA

CORDOBA

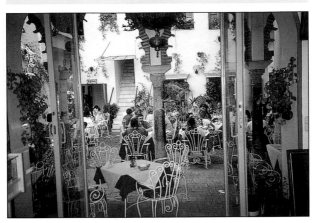

HOTEL GONZALEZ
~ TOWN HOUSE HOTEL ~

Manriquez 3, 14003 Cordoba
TEL 957 479 819 **FAX** 957 486 187

Hidden away in one of the narrow, white-washed streets in Córdoba's old Jewish quarter, just a stone's throw from the beautiful Mezquita, is this unusual little hotel, built in the remains of a 16thC Moorish palace. The only 'remains' we could see were a rectangular stone doorway and one stone capital, but Joaquín and Manuel González have added plenty of Moorish touches, such as arabesque arches on the patio. They also run a souvenir shop adjoining the hotel, full of gaudy Moorish vases, but this does not affect (or reflect) the character of the hotel, which is run with a happy blend of informality and efficiency.

Our first impression was of a cool marble interior and a charming receptionist. The hall leads through the arches to a lovely patio, packed with pretty red and white dining-tables and copious flowers and greenery. Geraniums hang down from every possible ledge and balcony. There is also a modern bar where breakfast is served. Upstairs, the bedrooms are simple and comfortable; most have small balconies looking over the patio. An (otherwise impressed) reader thought the food uninteresting and recommends El Churrasco, five minutes' walk away. Another (likewise impressed) reports night-time noise, possibly from a compressor. Another complained of heat in his bedroom, thin mattresses and uninterested reception staff.

~

Nearby Mezquita, Alcázar, old Jewish quarter
Location in quiet street behind Mezquita (best found on foot); no private car parking – public car park
Meals breakfast, lunch, dinner
Prices rooms €€-€€€; breakfast €; meals €€
Rooms 15 double, 2 single, 3 family rooms, all with bath; all rooms have central heating, air-conditioning, phone, satellite TV, radio **Facilities** dining-room/patio, sitting-room, cafeteria/bar, souvenir shop **Credit cards** AE, MC, V
Children welcome **Disabled** no special facilities **Pets** not accepted
Closed restaurant only Nov **Proprietor** Joaquín and Manuel González

CORDOBA

PALMA DEL RIO

HOSPEDERIA DE SAN FRANCISCO

~ CONVERTED MONASTERY ~

Avenida Pio XII, 14700, Palma del Rio, Córdoba
TEL & FAX (957) 710183

THIS 15THC FRANCISCAN MONASTERY stands on a small square at the centre of a confusing one-way system. If you get lost, don't hesitate to ask for directions; everyone knows where the Hospedería is, as it becomes a focus of attention at fiesta time (the staff dress up as monks and run a bar behind the church).

The Moreno family converted the monastery into a hotel five years ago. The care they took is immediately obvious as you enter the main courtyard; tables are set up in the cloisters, where you can watch pigeons nesting in the bell-tower as you eat. The main dining-room is a high-ceilinged hall, dominated by a huge fireplace. All the sitting areas are comfortable, especially the tiled bar, with its beamed ceiling and old paintings. Some of the bedrooms were once monks' cells and are fairly small and basic, but what they lack in luxuries they make up for in character, with beautifully hand-painted basins and bed-covers woven by local nuns.

Chef Iñaki has an excellent reputation, and his caricature (round, moustached and wagging a long finger) adorns the constantly changing menu, which reflects his Basque origins. A German reader reports poor service: a temporary failure, we hope. ~

NEARBY Córdoba (55 km); Seville (90 km); churches and palaces in Écija and Carmona.
LOCATION on quiet square in heart of town; car parking
MEALS breakfast, lunch, dinner
PRICES rooms €€-€€€€; breakfast €; lunch €€, dinner €€
ROOMS 14 double, one single, 2 family rooms, all with bath; all have central heating, air-conditioning, phone, TV, safe
FACILITIES dining-room, sitting-room, bar, patio, cloisters
CREDIT CARDS AE, DC, MC, V
CHILDREN welcome **DISABLED** no special facilities **PETS** accepted
CLOSED restaurant only, Sun dinner
MANAGER Iñaki Martínez

JAÉN

ÚBEDA

PT CONDESTABLE DAVALOS

~ TOWN MANSION ~

Plaza de Vázquez de Molina 1, 23400, Úbeda, Jaén
TEL (953) 750345 **FAX** (953) 751259

Somewhat overshadowed by the lovely façade of the 16thC chapel next door to it, Úbeda's stately Parador stands on the Renaissance square of Vázquez de Molina. Its internal courtyard is delightful; sixteen slender pillars (on both floors) enclose a stone-flagged patio set with tables and chairs. Striking blue-and-white patterned tiles half cover the walls around the outside. A sweeping staircase leads to the glass-enclosed gallery, past suits of armour and a spectacular light inside a double-headed glass eagle. Some bedrooms are around the gallery, others look on to smaller leafy quads or the ornamental garden. There is more attention to detail here than in the average Parador – carved bed-heads, hand-painted mirrors and wooden writing desks.

Guests have the choice of two bars, the underground taberna or a bar-cum-sitting-room on the way to the gardens. Red-tiled floors with little picture inlays are found in all public rooms, including the attractive dining-room. It is a friendly and animated place, in which it is easy to relax – perhaps in the shade of giant ferns In the courtyard, or under pine trees in the garden. It seemed half the size of its 31 rooms, without being cramped – a great base for exploring this historic town. 'Just sitting in the patio is worth the price – which is saying something,' writes a much-impressed U.S. reader.

~

Nearby Plaza, palaces, churches; Baeza (10 km); Jaén (55 km).
Location on square in historic part of town; follow signs; with car parking
Meals breakfast, lunch, dinner
Prices rooms €€€€; breakfast €; meals €€
Rooms 31 double, all with bath; all rooms have central heating, air-conditioning, phone, TV, minibar, hairdrier, radio
Facilities 2 dining-rooms, sitting-room, TV room, bar, cafeteria
Credit cards AE, DC, MC, V
Children welcome **Disabled** access difficult **Pets** not accepted, except guide dogs
Closed never **Manager** José Muñoz Romera

JAEN

ÚBEDA

PALACIO DE LA RAMBLA

~ ARISTOCRATIC MANSION ~

Plaza del Marqués 1, 23400, Úbeda, Jaén
TEL (953) 750196 **FAX** (953) 750267

There could be no more appropriate place to stay in the historic city of Úbeda than in this 16th century urban stately home, part of which has been opened to guests by the present Marquesa de la Rambla in order to help with the upkeep. More a seignorial guest house than a hotel, the door of the Palacio de la Rambla is kept locked and you have to summon the caretaker via an intercom.

The central feature is the patio, dripping with ivy, which is one of Úbeda's Renaissance treasures. Around it are the four original rooms which are decorated with old engravings and family antiques. One has an old-fashioned blue bath on legs; the other has its own fireplace. The two other rooms on the ground floor have less character. Another four rooms have been added upstairs at the front of the house.

Breakfast – 'whatever you want'– is brought to your room or served at one end of the salon. The grand piano at the other end holds the family photograph collection. 'Delightful'; 'warm and welcoming atmosphere' writes a recent visitor.

~

Nearby monuments of Úbeda; Baeza (11km); Cazorla Nature Reserve (55km).
Location in the town centre; 4 garage places available
Meals breakfast (other meals for groups only by prior arrangement)
Prices bed and breakfast €€€€
Rooms 7 double, 1 suite, all with bath; all rooms have central heating, TV, minibar, telephone
Facilities sitting-room
Credit cards AE, V
Children accepted
Disabled access difficult
Pets not accepted
Closed 15 Jul to 15 Aug
Proprietor Elena Meneses de Orozco

GRANADA

GRANADA

HOTEL AMÉRICA

~ TOWN HOUSE HOTEL ~

Real de la Alhambra 53, 18009, Granada
TEL (958) 227471 FAX (958) 227470
E-MAIL hamerica@moebius.es

Tucked away between the Alhambra and Granada's Parador (page 150), this delightful family-run hotel offers a perfect location at an affordable price. It is a small, friendly place, built around a vine-covered patio. In the summer months, the patio doubles as a dining-room – pretty tiled tables are set out, and you dine by the light of hanging lanterns to the sound of running water. The choice of dishes is limited, but everything is home-cooked, and if the smells coming from the kitchen when we visited are anything to go by, the food is delicious; it is also reasonably priced.

The bedrooms are small but comfortable and clean, and overlook either the patio or the gardens of the Alhambra. They are brightened up by colourful woven bedspreads and curtains. The sitting area next to the reception is crammed with pottery, ornaments, screens, sofas and rocking chairs – leaving hardly enough room to sit down. It is a small, busy hotel, and not the kind of place you would want to linger in all day. But with the Alhambra on your doorstep, there is more than enough to keep you busy. 'A friendly, but casual welcome,' says a recent reporter. Popular with our German readers.

~

Nearby Alhambra, Generalife and gardens, cathedral; Sierra Nevada (35 km), Costa del Sol (65 km).
Location inside walls of Alhambra (follow road past entrance); car parking not allowed in square. Use Alhambra car park (15 mins walk) – reduced fee.
Meals breakfast, lunch, dinner
Prices rooms €€-€€€, breakfast €; meals €€
Rooms 8 double, one family room, all with bath; 4 single, 2 with bath, 2 with shower; all rooms have central heating, phone
Facilities dining-room, sitting-room
Credit cards MC, V
Children accepted **Disabled** one ground-floor room **Pets** not accepted
Closed 1 Dec to 28 Feb **Proprietor** Rafael Garzón

GRANADA

GRANADA

PT SAN FRANCISCO
～ CONVERTED CONVENT PARADOR ～

Real de la Alhambra, 18009, Granada
TEL (958) 221440 **FAX** (958) 222264

'Book at least three months in advance' was the advice that the management of this extremely popular Parador asked us to pass on; 'and more in high season', we would add. The attraction of this converted 14thC convent, set in the gardens of the famous Alhambra, is easy to see – especially when the day-trippers have disappeared – and the results are predictable.

Although the hotel is rather big and impersonal, it has some lovely touches – the chapel where Isabella of Spain was originally buried, now open to the sky, is used as a patio, and the adjoining courtyard full of plants and flowers is a place to sit and relax in lovely old rocking-chairs. Alcoves in the corridors and stairways are decorated with carved wooden figures of saints, and the stone-flagged floors are covered in bright Granadan rugs. The bedrooms are fairly standard, with large, tiled bathrooms; 32 of them have superb views over the Alhambra and the Generalife. Public rooms are comfortable, and there are seating areas on the terraces. The dining-room gets very busy – but any hotel near the Alhambra attracts crowds, and at least here you can sit and wait in glorious surroundings.

～

Nearby Alhambra, Generalife and gardens, cathedral; Sierra Nevada (35 km), Costa del Sol (65 km).
Location in Alhambra gardens (follow road past entrance); with garden and garage for 17 cars
Meals breakfast, lunch, dinner
Prices rooms €€€€; breakfast €; meals €€
Rooms 35 double, 3 single, all with bath; all rooms have central heating, air-conditioning, phone, TV, minibar, hairdrier
Facilities dining-room, sitting-room, bar
Credit cards AE, DC, MC, V
Children welcome **Disabled** some ground-floor rooms **Pets** not accepted
Closed never **Manager** Juan Antonio Gianello

GRANADA

GRANADA

PALACIO DE SANTA INÉS
~ TOWN HOUSE HOTEL ~

Cuesta de Santa Inés, 9, 18010, Granada
TEL (958) 222362 **FAX** (958) 222465

The problem with staying on the Alhambra hill is that it's hard to escape from the thousands of fellow tourists. Consider instead basing yourself in the Albaicín, the mysterious, whitewashed Moorish quarter that tumbles down the hillside opposite.

Here you'll find the Palacio de Santa Inès, a 16thC mansion that manages to be both grand yet intimate, and combines the old and the new to great effect. Its centrepiece is its enclosed patio, where half-revealed frescoes - said to be by a student of Raphael - and marble pillars are offset by chic soft furnishings. Upstairs, wooden galleries decorated with modern art lead to

Striking, beamed bedrooms, furnished with wrought-iron beds and more art. Standard double rooms are generally small, however, so it might be worth splashing out on a suite. The grandest (the Alhambra) has a fabulous mudèjar ceiling, while others have roof terraces with sensational views of the Alhambra over the Albaicìnis jumble of terracotta roofs.

A reader writes of a badly bungled reservation and a poor breakfast – one-off failings, we hope. Reports especially welcome.
~

NEARBY Albaicìn; Alhambra a 10-minute walk away.
LOCATION up a quiet back alley 200 yards from the main Plaza Nueva; parking 5-minute walk away in public car park
MEALS breakfast
PRICES rooms €€€-€€€€; breakfast €
ROOMS 6 double, 7 suites, all with bath; all rooms have central heating, TV (satellite), phone, air-conditioning, minibar; suites have kitchenettes
FACILITIES breakfast room, sitting-room
CREDIT CARDS AE, DC, M, V
CHILDREN welcome **DISABLED** no special facilities **PETS** small dogs
CLOSED never
OWNER Nicolas Garrido Berastegui

GRANADA

ORGIVA

HOTEL TARAY

~ COUNTRY HOTEL ~

Ctra. Tablate-Albunol, Km 18, 18400 Orgiva (Granada)
TEL (958) 784 525 **FAX** (958) 784 531
E-MAIL tarayalp@teleline.es

Even by local standards, the Taray has a great location. The single-storey building is on a shelf high in a steep valley of the Alpujarra mountains, with a terrific outlook over the fertile river plain below and beautiful, barren sierras beyond. It's on the edge of the market town of Orgiva, in well-planted gardens, with a river nearby. A London reader noted the friendly reception and 'pleasant service', spacious public rooms and adequate bedrooms. Whitewashed walls and terracotta floors dominate the interior, predictably, but happily. Food, from the hotel's own farm, is 'good but not exceptional'. The bedrooms, some with their own sitting-rooms and private terraces, are spread along a common terrace which in turn gives on to the lawns. Walk through the gardens to a pond with turtles and ducks to find the large swimming-pool with a generous shallow area for children. A reliable, reasonably-priced base for exploring the Alpujarra and its villages.

~

Nearby Cave country, Granada
Location on southern outskirts of Orgiva, own grounds and car parking
Meals breakfast, lunch, dinner
Prices €€
Rooms 27; 12 double, 15 in cottages in grounds, all with air-conditioning, TV, heating, minibar
Facilities TV/music room, cafe-bar, two dining rooms, garden, swimming-pool
Credit cards AC, DC, MC, V
Children welcome
Disabled some rooms suitable
Pets not accepted
Closed never
Proprietor Eladio Cuadros

GRANADA

BUBION

VILLA TURISTICA DE BUBION

~ TOURIST VILLAGE ~

Barrio Alto s/n, Bubión, Granada
TEL (958) 763111 FAX (958) 763136
E-MAIL albujarr@ctb.es WEBSITE www.ctb.es.albujarr

This is the first in a new concept of accommodation in Andalucia: a cluster of self-contained apartments built in the local style. The Villa Turística, run by a co-operative, recreates the architectural atmosphere of an Alpujarran village with its low-rise, flat topped houses, singular chimneys and shady alleyways. Compare it to the real thing in Bubión only a stone's throw down the hill.

There are three models of apartment, the largest having two bedrooms, two bathrooms and a sitting/dining room. All are decorated similarly, using local textiles and ceramics. Each has a fireplace – vital in the Alpujarras in winter – which room service will attend to. When we inspected, the authenticity of the rooms was only let down by the veneered kitchen cabinets, which we understand are being replaced.

The central block near the car-park houses reception, the dining-room/bar and a rather impersonal sitting-room upstairs – the sofas in front of reception are more inviting.

On weekdays the manager offers a reduced price to readers who present a copy of this guide.

~

Nearby walks in the Alpujarras; Bubión; Capileira (2km); the Veleta, by unsurfaced road to over 3,000 metres (25km).
Location above the village; car parking and garden
Meals breakfast, lunch, dinner
Prices rooms €€€; breakfast €; meals €€
Rooms 43 apartments, all with bath; all rooms have fireplace, TV, fridge, telephone
Facilities sitting-room, dining room, bar; mountain bikes
Credit cards AE, DC, MC, V
Children accepted
Disabled easy access **Pets** accepted at extra charge
Closed never
Manager Victor Fernandez

GRANADA

LA BOBADILLA

~ ANDALUCIAN VILLA ~

Finca La Bobadilla, 18300, Loja, Granada
TEL (958) 321861 **FAX** (958) 321810
E-MAIL info@la-bobadilla.com **WEBSITE** www.la-bobadilla.com

Arches, tiles, white walls, iron grilles, fountains, plants, patios and balconies: La Bobadilla resembles a labyrinthine Andalucian village, set in its own 350-hectare grove of olives and evergreen oaks. More than one visitor has described it as the best hotel in Spain, indeed as one of the best in Europe and an inspection visit before this edition went to press confirmed that standards remain as high as ever.

There are 60 rooms: but what rooms. Most of them are enormous, with private garden or terrace. Every room is decorated with an abundance of marbles, silks and woodwork. The columns of the main hall are reminiscent of the mosque at Cordoba. There are concerts in the hotel chapel.

For outdoor entertainment, there is archery and clay-pigeon shooting; or you can ride, or drive a 4x4, through the olive groves. If you are still in need of variety, you can relax in the Turkish baths. There is not a corner, patio or corridor which does not boast some atmospheric detail: splashes of greenery, the gurgles of water seem to greet you at every turn. 'An incredible hotel' writes a well-travelled visitor, 'but we thought, given the sky-high prices, the food at both restaurants was disappointing.'

~

Nearby Archidona (18km); Antequera (35 km); Granada (70 km).
Location 3 km on the C334 from Salinas to Iznajar; car parking
Meals breakfast, lunch, dinner
Prices rooms ⓔⓔⓔⓔ, breakfast ⓔⓔ; meals ⓔⓔⓔ
Rooms 49 double (29 with sitting room), 2 single, 9 suites, all with bath; all rooms have air- conditioning, phone, minibar, TV (satellite)
Facilities 2 restaurants, bar, meeting room; 2 swimming- pools, terrace, sauna, Turkish baths, massage; tennis-court, mountain bikes; shops, chapel, beauty salon, hairdressers
Credit cards AE, DC, MC, V
Children accepted **Disabled** 2 rooms with special facilities **Pets** only in rooms
Closed never **Manager** Miguel del Valle

ALMERIA

SAN JOSÉ

SAN JOSÉ
~ BEACH HOTEL ~

Correo s/n, 04118, San José Almería
TEL (950) 380116

Spain's extreme south-east corner has escaped the excesses of package holiday tourism and this hotel is ideally located to enjoy some of the last unspoilt beaches on the Mediterranean coast.

The house, reminiscent of a Swiss chalet, was formerly a warehouse for *esparto* – a grass traditionally used to make shoes and baskets.

Large semi-circular windows illuminate the sitting-room and allow you to look down on the beach or gaze out to sea. The whole place is full of entertaining details. A parrot in a large cage on a pedestal is kept covered up to stop it talking. Beyond the dining-room an intimate salon has a rustic cot, an old barber's chair and a collection of sea urchins and shells.

The best bedrooms are the two on the second floor facing the sea. All the rooms have character with their antique tiled floors and colonial ceiling fans. But the enormous bathrooms are marred by their antiquated plumbing and fittings – which may convince you that the hotel is overpriced.

Tourists fill San José in the summer months. In the winter the place is dead, or peaceful, as you prefer, but the climate is still warm and sunny.

~

Nearby Cabo de Gata nature reserve; Almería (40km).
Location on the beach in San José; garden and car parking
Meals breakfast, lunch, dinner
Prices rooms €€€-€€€€; breakfast €; meals €€
Rooms 8 double with bath; all rooms have ceiling fan, safe, TV
Facilities dining-room, bar, meeting rooms; terrace, private beach, solarium, sitting-room
Credit cards MC, V
Children accepted
Disabled access difficult
Pets not accepted
Closed Oct to Mar **Manager** Eduardo G. Zárate

ALMERIA

PECHINA

BALNEARIO DE SIERRA ALHAMILLA

〜 SPA HOTEL 〜

04259, Pechina, Almería
TEL (950) 317413 **FAX** (950) 160257

Nothing could be more relaxing after a day in the car than to slip into this spa hotel's heated swimming-pool with its underwater massage jets.

Inside the hotel you can shut yourself away from the bleak surroundings of arid mountains and relax in modest comfort. Peace reigns day and night: the only sound in the patio is the trickle of a fountain.

The original building was raised in 1777 by the Bishop of Almeria on the site of Roman baths. A few years ago the ruins were faithfully reconstructed by the present owner, the polite and quietly-spoken Isidro Pérez.

The dining-room is in a barrel-vaulted chamber decorated with patterned tiles and Mudejar plasterwork. The food is well-intentioned and daintily presented on octagonal plates but not of outstanding quality. Breakfast is served under the brick dome of the Bishop's former chapel, looked down upon by an altarpiece.

The bedrooms are old-fashioned with double doors and arched ceilings. Some of the bathrooms suffer from a few niggling, though unimportant, defects.

〜

Nearby Las Millares neolithic necropolis (20km); Mini-Hollywood film sets (22km); solar power station (35km).
Location turn off N 340 for Chuche; hotel is signposted from Pechina; car parking
Meals breakfast, lunch, dinner
Prices rooms €€-€€€; breakfast €; meals €€
Rooms 16 double, 8 suites, all with bath; all rooms have central heating, TV, telephone
Facilities sitting-room, dining- room, breakfast room, spa facilities, heated swiming-pool
Credit cards AE, MC, V
Children accepted **Disabled** easy access **Pets** not accepted
Closed never **Proprietor** Isidro Pérez

CADIZ

ARCOS DE LA FRONTERA

CASA DEL CORREGIDOR

~ TOWN HOUSE PARADOR ~

Plaza de España, 11630, Arcos de la Frontera, Cádiz
TEL (956) 700500 FAX (956) 701116
E-MAIL arcos@parador.es

A WHITE MANSION on the edge of a formidable cliff. Flower-patterned tiles border the white walls along the corridors; ceramic pictures tell the stories of bullfights; and potted plants fill the pebbled internal courtyard. Eight of the rooms enjoy views over the patchwork of fields and orchards far below. Some of the others look onto the main square of Arcos and the lovely 16thC church of Santa María.

Both the bar and dining-room have French windows opening on to large sunny cliff-top terraces. Order the *menu degustación* to sample a range of regional specialities.

~

NEARBY Jerez (30 km); Cádiz (63km); Grazalema (50 km).
LOCATION on main square, next to Santa Maria (follow Parador signs); with car parking in square
MEALS breakfast, lunch, dinner
PRICES rooms ©©©-©©©©; breakfast ©; meals ©©
ROOMS 20 double, 4 single, all with bath; all rooms have central heating, air-conditioning, phone, TV, minibar, radio
FACILITIES dining-room, 2 sitting-rooms, bar, 2 terraces
CREDIT CARDS AE, DC, MC, V **CHILDREN** accepted **DISABLED** lift/elevator
PETS not accepted **CLOSED** never **MANAGER** Máximo Pérez

PARADORES IN ANDALUCIA

The two Paradores in Huelva are both modern. The 35-room PT Costa de la Luz at Ayamonte, on the borders of Portugal, is a sprawling white building high above the city, with magnificent views (Tel (959) 256422). Cádiz has a large modern Parador, a six-storey white complex called the Atlántico, on the south side of the isthmus. Ask for a room with a sea view (Tel (956) 226905).

The Costa del Sol has three Paradores. Two are close to Málaga – as well as the PT de Gibralfaro (see page 176) there is the self-explanatory Golf, a little way west of the town (Tel (952) 381255). The third is at Nerja: large and modern but attractive, with well-furnished rooms and an elevator down to the beach (Tel (95) 2520050). North-east of Almería is PT Reyes Católicos at Mojácar (Tel (950) 478250), which feels more intimate than its 98 rooms would suggest.

Inland, the Paradores at Antequera, Arcos de la Frontera, Carmona, Granada, Jaén and Úbeda have detailed entries. The modern 83-room PT de la Arruzafa at Córdoba is 3 km from the middle of the city (Tel (957) 275900). The dismal PT de Bailén has little to recommend it apart from its pool (Tel (953) 670100). Much more appealing is the PT El Adelantado at Cazorla – (Tel (953) 727075).

CADIZ

ARCOS DE LA FRONTERA

EL CONVENTO
～ CONVERTED CONVENT ～

Calle Maldonado 2, 11630, Arcos de la Frontera, Cádiz
TEL (956) 702333 **FAX** (956) 704128

We have long counted this hotel, in part of a convent in the old town of Arcos, as one of our favourites in Andalucia. Readers have subsequently confirmed this judgement: a recent reporter says it would 'live long in any visitor's memory'; the only carping note is from those who notice its inclination for self-congratulation. Extensive changes have been made to provide more spacious public areas and a café.

Certainly the owners, José Antonio Roldán and his wife María Moreno, could not be more welcoming; but neither does Sr Roldán miss an opportunity to promote his enterprise. The restaurant walls (and others) display numerous press cuttings.

The bedrooms are homely, and sometimes decorated with ingenuous taste. Each year one of them is formally dedicated to a 'famous' son of Arcos. Six of the rooms have terraces and most enjoy panoramic views to rival those of the nearby Parador. Breakfast is served in the convent's former sacristy – a white arched chamber – and there is bar service during the day. For other meals you have to stroll round to the Roldán's garlanded restaurant, one minute's walk away, in the attractive 16th century Valdespino palace. Specialities include asparagus soup, partridge in almond sauce and home-made desserts.

～

Nearby churches of Santa María and San Pedro; Jerez (30 km).
Location on a tiny back street, past church and Parador; car parking in main square
Meals breakfast, lunch, dinner
Prices rooms €€-€€€; breakfast €; meals €€
Rooms 10 double, 1 single, all with bath; all rooms have central heating, air-conditioning, phone, satellite TV, hairdrier
Facilities 2 dining-rooms, bar, 2 terraces
Credit cards AE, DC, MC, V **Children** welcome **Disabled** access difficult
Pets not accepted **Closed** never **Proprietor** María Moreno

CADIZ

ARCOS DE LA FRONTERA

HOTEL LOS OLIVOS

~ TOWN HOTEL ~

Paseo de Boliches 30, 11630, Arcos de la Frontera, Cádiz
TEL (956) 700811 **FAX** (956) 702018

The receptionist at the Olivos told us (in good English) that the hotel is usually full; it is easy to see why. It is an attractive place, even from the outside – built in typical Arcos style with whitewashed walls, yellow tiled roofs and iron grills over the windows, and equipped with pots of geraniums on arched balconies. But it is the interior that really captivates.

The rooms are built around an internal courtyard; café- style tables and chairs are set out in the middle, under a palm tree. The breakfast room is decorated in the same dark green furniture and doubles up as a bar; it looks on to a tiny patio containing an old stone well. Behind the glass arches surrounding the courtyard is a cosy alcove with wicker sofas and armchairs, and bowls of fresh flowers.

The bedrooms are light and airy – comfortable, but not cluttered with furniture. All have different cane bedsteads, pale covers and curtains, and mats covering stone-tiled floors. The two front bedrooms have balconies with sweeping views over the plains and the nearby olive-groves from which the hotel takes its name.

~

Nearby churches of Santa María and San Pedro, castle; Jerez, Cádiz, Ronda within driving distance.
Location on road up to Parador, overlooking Guada-lete plains; car parking in garage (Pts 700 per 24 hours)
Meals breakfast
Prices rooms €-€€; breakfast €
Rooms 17 double, 2 single; all with bath; all rooms have central heating, air-conditioning, phone, TV, minibar, radio
Facilities sitting-rooms, TV room, bar/breakfast room
Credit cards AE, DC, MC, V
Children welcome **Disabled** ground floor rooms **Pets** not accepted **Closed** never
Proprietor Raquel Roldán

CADIZ

ARCOS DE LA FRONTERA

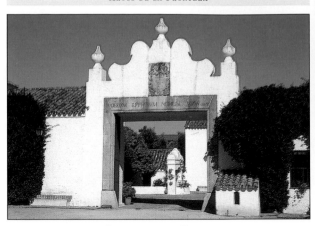

CORTIJO FAIN
~ ANDALUCIAN VILLA ~

11630, Arcos de la Frontera Cádiz.
TEL & FAX (956) 701167

This landowner's residence, or cortijo, stands in the middle of a vast olive grove not far from one of the most spectacular of the White Towns. The silence is only broken by the odd tractor ploughing between the trees.

The house and outbuildings enclose a pretty courtyard with a well and drinking trough in the middle. Most of the rooms are upstairs in the main house. They are of varying shapes and sizes but all warmly furnished with antiques, iron or brass bedsteads, crocheted bedspreads, books and flowers. On the first-floor landing is a small household chapel.

Equally inviting are the rustically decorated public rooms littered with oil paintings and more antiques. The cafeteria is in the old stables. From the sitting-room, a door leads into the library: an even more relaxing room lined with 7,000 leather-bound volumes. The dining room has a glass-enclosed porch opening on to the garden.

From the back of the house a path leads across the lawn between the olive trees to a large, curving swimming-pool crossed by a hump-backed bridge.

~

Nearby Arcos de la Frontera (3km); Grazalema (53km). Carretera de Algar, Km 3,
Location from Arcos take the road towards El Algar and turn off left (signposted) after 3 km; garden and car parking
Meals breakfast, lunch, dinner
Prices rooms €€-€€€€; breakfast €; meals €
Rooms 3 double, 1 single, 4 suites, one apartment, all with bath; all rooms have air-conditioning, radiator
Facilities dining-room, sitting-room, bar, swimming-pool
Credit cards AE, MC, V
Children welcome **Disabled** 3 ground floor rooms **Pets** accepted **Closed** never
Proprietor José Luis Jiménez Rodriguez

CADIZ

ARCOS DE LA FRONTERA

HACIENDA EL SANTISCAL
~ COUNTRY HOUSE HOTEL ~

Avda. El Santiscal, 129 (Iago de Arcos), 11630 Arcos de la Frontera, Cadiz
TEL (956) 708 313 **FAX** (956) 708 268
E-MAIL santisal@gadesinfo.com

This has been a regrettable ommission from earlier editions of the guide, but we're pleased, on the recommendation of Jenny Rees, author of our *Southern France* and *Ireland* guides, to include it in this new edition. It's a well-restored, dignified, whitewashed 15thC manor house – but that's only the start. Jenny was struck by its lovely position, with views over the nearby lake, and of nearby Arcos; and by the charm of its owners, Hussein, an Egyptian, and his Andalucian wife, Franchesca. They also have a restaurant in Arcos, which, along with the Hacienda, of course, is supplied with fresh vegetables and herbs from the Hacienda's garden. The public spaces are decorated in authentic Hacienda style, offering the understated good taste that we value much more than plush smartness. The conservatory eating area is a particularly charming, somewhat unusual structure. Bedrooms are of a similar standard, all individual, air-conditioned, and with views of the lake or hills. For amusement, there's the (circular) swimming pool, riding, biking or walking.

Nearby Arcos; Jerez, Gibraltar, Ronda, Malaga and Seville within driving distance.
Location ten minutes from Arcos, signposted from the the N-342 outside the town; in own grounds with private car parking
Meals breakfast, lunnch, dinner
Price €€€
Rooms 11 double, 1 suite, all with bath, heating, air-conditioning.
Facilities sitting-room, dining-room, bar, gardens, swimming-pool.
Credit cards AE, DC, MC, V
Children welcome
Disabled not suitable
Pets only small dogs by agreement in advance
Closed never
Proprietors Franchesca Gallardo Carrasco

CADIZ

CONVENTO DE SAN FRANCISCO

~ CONVERTED CONVENT ~

La Plazuela, 11150, Vejer de la Frontera, Cádiz
TEL (956) 451001 **FAX** (956) 451004

Vejer is a delightful medieval town crowning a solitary hill near the coast. In the old part of town, the Felipe brothers have lovingly converted a 17thC convent into an unusual hotel; a set of photographs in the echoing *taberna* tell the story of the renovations. Many of the remains have been preserved – a Roman mosaic in the hall, a cabinet of medieval pottery on the stairs, the old choir stalls and frescos in the sitting-room. The bedrooms still have their original stone arches visible in the walls and the furniture has been designed in harmony – arched bed-heads, stripped pine desks, wooden shutters. The result is effective – the simplicity of a nun's cell with the facilities of a modern hotel.

The refectory still serves as a dining-room, still with wooden benches and tables lining the walls. Bright modern cushions and abstract modern paintings add a splash of colour. Our inspector's meal, the *menu del dia*, was excellent, piping hot and served by cheerful staff. Outside the dining-room is an obscure metal sculpture, two floors high. The centre-piece of the Convento is the 'choir hall' – a great place to sit when the sun filters through the windows in the early morning.

~

Nearby Castle, churches, Jewish Quarter.
Location on small square in old part of town, round corner from main street on cliff edge; car parking on main street
Meals breakfast, lunch, dinner
Prices rooms €€-€€€; breakfast €; menu €€
Rooms 18 double, 5 single, one family room; all with bath; all rooms have electric heating, phone, TV
Facilities dining-room, sitting-room, cafeteria, bar
Credit cards DC, MC, V
Children welcome **Disabled** lift/elevator **Pets** not accepted **Closed** never
Manager Jesús Felipe Gallego

CADIZ

La Almoraima

CASA CONVENTO

~ CONVERTED CONVENT ~

La Almoraima, 11350, Castellar de la Frontera, Cádiz
TEL (956) 693002 **FAX** (956) 693214

Opposite a large factory on the main road to Jimena, a small sign points up a wooded drive to the Casa Convento. Following the road, you pass from scrubby trees dotted with nesting boxes to beautiful landscaped gardens, and end up in front of the yellow and white façade of a 17thC convent. Tall palm trees shade the arched windows and elegant pillars along the front of the building. The place is serene – it comes as quite a surprise to discover that until recently it was a hunting lodge (witness the mounted hunting trophies in the public rooms).

Despite its grandiose appearance, the hotel is surprisingly informal and relaxed; the public rooms are obviously used, not just admired. The 'bar' consists of a trolley of spirits, the 'games room' a billiard table, the 'music room' a mini grand piano, and the 'library' a couple of ancient book shelves. The rooms upstairs are reminiscent of an English country house – with tapestries on the sitting-room walls and chandeliers over the long dining-room table. Bedrooms are comfortable, overlooking either the gardens or the central courtyard. The chapel and the old bell-towers are the only reminders that this was once a convent.

~

Nearby Castellar de la Frontera; Algeciras (25 km).
Location in wooded grounds, 12 km north of Algeciras on N340; with gardens and car parking
Meals breakfast, lunch, dinner
Prices rooms €€-€€€€; breakfast €; meals €€
Rooms 7 double, 4 single; all with bath; all rooms have central heating, phone; most rooms have fires, some rooms have TV
Facilities dining room, sitting-room, games room; swimming-pool, tennis court, mini-golf, horse riding
Credit cards AE, DC, MC, V
Children not accepted **Disabled** access difficult **Pets** accepted in bedrooms
Closed never **Manager** Juan Montoya

CADIZ

SANLUCAR DE BARRAMEDA

POSADA DE PALACIO

~ TOWN HOUSE ~

Calle Caballeros 11, 11540, Sanlúcar de Barrameda, Cádiz
TEL (956) 364840 **FAX** (956) 365060
WEBSITE www.madeinspain.net

Antonio and Renata Navarrete set up this pension in 1986, when they moved from Switzerland. It is a typical Andalucian town house, near the Bombadilla sherry bodegas in the old part of the town. If you get lost, follow your nose; an overpowering smell of Sanlúcar's famous manzanilla lingers around the warehouses.

The guest-house is built around a courtyard of original stone floor-tiles. Most of the bedrooms are in this part of the building, including two ground-floor suites. All the rooms are clean and comfortable – and unconventional, adding to their charm. Those we saw were very spacious – we had a cavernous bathroom, even bigger than our bedroom. We ate a superb home-made breakfast in our room overlooking the tiny garden.

The public rooms are full of interesting objects that the couple have collected over the years; an old grinding wheel hangs next to modern film posters in the bar, miniature pictures decorate the walls, and fresh flowers abound. You are constantly reminded that this is a home as well as a hotel. Tables are set outside under the wistaria, and up ivy-covered steps, four new rooms look on to a large stone sun-terrace. 'Truly enchanting', says a reader.

~

Nearby Castle, palace, sherry bodegas, beach.
Location near castle and palace, in old part of town; car parking on street
Meals breakfast, dinner
Prices rooms €€; breakfast €; dinner €€
Rooms 8 double, 4 with bath, 4 with shower, 2 single with bath, 3 suites, with bath; all rooms have phone
Facilities sitting-room, TV room, bar/breakfast room, terrace, dining-room
Credit cards MC, V
Children welcome **Disabled** ground-floor rooms
Pets accepted **Closed** Jan and Feb
Proprietors Antonio and Renata Navarrete

CADIZ

SANLUCAR DE BARRAMEDA

TARTANEROS

~ TOWN HOTEL ~

Calle Tartaneros 8, 11540, Sanlúcar de Barrameda, Cádiz
TEL (956) 362044 FAX (956) 360045

MOST OF THE GROUND FLOOR of the Tartaneros is given over to an elegant *art nouveau* cafeteria spreading through various drawing rooms, rich in ornamental period detail.

The hotel, reached through a door beside the bar, is less distinguished but also furnished with eclectic taste. The large open-plan sitting-room is littered with maritime memorabilia and other curios including a bullfighter's suit of lights.

The bedrooms are dotted with antique furniture. Those on the ground floor are in the vaults of old wine cellar. The upstairs rooms are bigger.

~

NEARBY palace, sherry bodegas; Jerez de la Frontera (22km).
LOCATION in the city centre; no garden or car parking
MEALS breakfast
PRICES rooms €€; breakfast €
ROOMS 18 double, 4 single, all with bath; all rooms have central heating, air-conditioning, TV, minibar, telephone, safe
FACILITIES cafeteria, sitting-room
CREDIT CARDS AE, DC, MC, V
CHILDREN accepted
DISABLED easy access to ground floor rooms
PETS small ones only **CLOSED** never **PROPRIETOR** Enrique Pérez

CADIZ

TARIFA

HURRICANE
~ BEACH HOTEL ~

Carretera de Málaga a Cádiz, 11380, Tarifa
TEL (956) 684919 **FAX** (956) 680329

Well-heeled thirtysomethings make up the clientele of the hip and casual Hurricane Hotel. Its name more than hints at the prime attraction. Strong winds make the southern end of the Costa de la Luz the best windsurfing spot in mainland Europe, and you can learn to ride or hire a board at the windsurfing school right next to the hotel.

The Hurricane's snazzy gym and riding stables also lure sporty landlubbers, and the hotel offers many enticements for indolent types too. A gorgeous palm, hibiscus and eucalyptus filled garden envelops two swimming-pools (one set aside for adults only), and leads to a narrow but pretty and secluded sandy beach. The Spanish/Italian food has a good reputation, especially for its fish dishes. When it's warm, dinners are served under towering Moorish arches on a romantic terrace overlooking the main pool, and the beach café does excellent salads and pastas for lunch.

Standard bedrooms are simple but tasteful; avoid those facing inland as they suffer from their proximity to the busy main road. Suites are worth paying extra for. They either come with private gardens, or are grand and exotic – maybe with keyhole arches over the bath and bold pictures of tigers on the walls.

~

Nearby Tarifa (7km); Bolonia Roman ruins (16km); Gibraltar (50km).
Location Between N340 coastal road and beach, 7km northwest of Tarifa; ample parking
Meals breakfast, lunch, dinner
Prices rooms €€-€€€€, including breakfast; meals €€-€€€€
Rooms 28 double, 6 suites, all with bath; all rooms have central heating, phone, air-conditioning, minibar; suites have TV
Facilities 2 bars, dining-room, 2 swimming-pools, gym, sauna, windsurfing, horse riding, mountain bikes **Credit cards** AE, DC, M, V **Children** welcome
Disabled limited access **Pets** accepted **Closed** never
Owner Michael Whaley

MALAGA

Hotels on the Costa del Sol

'Charming' and 'small' are not the first adjectives that spring to mind when considering hotels along the Costa del Sol. It has taken some searching to find such places along this 200 km holiday playground, and many of the hotels we describe in detail are not actually on the coast but behind it, hidden away in the mountains. Anyone who wants to be on the coast itself might consider some of the hotels listed below. A word of warning though: most of them get booked up in high season, so plan well in advance.

Tarifa – an unspoilt fishing village 22 km south-west of Algeciras – is not technically part of the Costa del Sol, but the 33-room Hurricane (Tel (956) 684919), is a paradise for wind-surfers and outdoor types.

The pick of Gibraltar's hotels is the Rock (Tel (350) 73000), a large, rather old-fashioned establishment serving traditional British food.

Just outside San Pedro de Alcántara is the Cortijo de los Caballos (Tel (952) 886767), a complex of 9 bungalow apartments around a swimming-pool and one of the few places in Spain not to accept children.

The true heart of the Costa del Sol is Marbella, the most up-market of the resorts. One of the more stylish places to stay here is the Marbella Club (Tel (952) 822211) which is set in luxuriant gardens.

Further round the coast, after the package holiday resorts of Fuengirola and Torremolinos, comes Málaga. More than an airport it is a sprawling city which is best avoided in high season. If you have to stay here, the Palacio – luxurious, with a roof-top pool (Tel (952) 215185) – and Casa Curro (Tel (952) 227200) – central, comfortable – are good alternatives to the Parador. Most hotels run a bus service to the airport.

East of Málaga the coast is less built up. The famous view from the Balcón de Europa, in Nerja, is definitely worth stopping for.

The 47-room Los Fenicios (Tel (958) 827900), in the small resort of La Herradura stands out from the blocks around it because of its original architecture and its unusual brass and glass lift.

The holiday strip terminates in the dry province of Almeria. In the city of the same name, the Torreluz IV (Tel (950) 234999) is brashly modern but distinguished by white leather sofas, a spiral staircase and a roof-top swimming pool.

HOTEL PRICES

As we explain in the introduction, many hotels did not know their future prices when we were preparing this edition. It is always wise to check when making a booking or checking in. Note that most hotels quote their rates excluding VAT (IVA in Spanish – usually 6%).

MALAGA

HOTEL MIAMI

~ TOWN HOUSE HOTEL ~

Calle Aladino 14, 29620, Torremolinos, Málaga
TEL (952) 385255 FAX (952) 053447
E-MAIL jmdejens@teleline.es

Somewhere in the ocean of concrete formed by the merger of Málaga and Torremolinos, a small sign directs you off the main coast road to the Miami. It is set in its own rounded driveway and is completely walled off from its surroundings – it feels just like an island. The house was built by Picasso's cousin as a holiday villa and has made an unusual hotel, set around a lagoon-like swimming pool. Palms and banana trees overshadow the pool and give it an exotic, tropical feel – you could be in the Caribbean rather than in the heart of Torremolinos, only yards away from a crowded beach and busy sea-front.

Some of the bedrooms are in need of attention; ours was worn and dusty, but adequate. Most have balconies, and all are cool and airy. One of the key features of the hotel is the grotto-like sitting-room, with its mixture of square and round windows peeping out of pebble-dashed walls and its curious fireplace of piled stones. It is full of interesting objects – animal-skin seats, copper pots, pilot lanterns.

There is no restaurant, but the Miami does serve probably the only 'Spanish' breakfast in Torremolinos – on the terrace above the pool.

~

Nearby beach; Málaga (15 km), Marbella (45 km).
Location on quiet side-street, 50 m from beach; signed
from main road through Torremolinos; with garden and ample car parking in drive
Meals breakfast
Prices rooms €-€€; breakfast €
Rooms 23 double, 3 single, all with bath; all rooms have central heating, phone, safe
Facilities sitting-room, breakfast room, bar/ patio, swimming-pool
Credit cards not accepted
Children accepted; play area **Disabled** 6 ground-floor rooms
Pets accepted **Closed** never
Manager Mercedes Gómez

MALAGA

ANTEQUERA

PT DE ANTEQUERA

MODERN PARADOR

Paseo García del Olmo, 29200, Antequera, Málaga
TEL (952) 840261 **FAX** (952) 841312

Although it is large and modern, this was one of our favourite Paradors, with exceptionally welcoming and helpful staff (so often the Parador weakness). It is set on a hill, overlooking plains and mountains and the pretty white town of Antequera. The two wings of the white building look on to a magnificent swimming-pool, surrounded by lawns and shady trees. Most bedrooms face this way, and have either direct access to the gardens or balconies overlooking them. The rooms are large, cool and comfortable, and have the most powerful showers in Spain.

The dining-room and split-level sitting-room are reminiscent of an Alpine chalet – add snow to the craggy mountain tops seen through the large windows, and you could be in Switzerland. The food, however, is definitely Spanish – delicious shellfish, local trout, paella, almond tarts. All the public rooms are large and formal; sofas, rocking-chairs and card tables are set out as if they were on display, not in use. Yet the atmosphere in the rest of the Parador is relaxed and informal (although one visitor's peace was marred by the presence of a conference group). An excellent base for exploring the surrounding countryside and the fascinating prehistoric monuments in the town.

Nearby Roman remains, castle; Costa del Sol (50 km).
Location on hill on edge of town; with gardens and car parking
Meals breakfast, lunch, dinner
Prices rooms €€-€€€, breakfast €; meals €€
Rooms 55 double, all with bath; all rooms have central heating, air-conditioning, phone, TV, minibar
Facilities dining-room, 2 sitting-rooms, bar; swimming-pool
Credit cards AE, DC, MC, V
Children welcome **Disabled** ground-floor rooms
Pets not accepted **Closed** never
Manager Manuel Martínez

MALAGA

RONDA

HOTEL SAN GABRIEL

∽ TOWN HOTEL ∽

Calle Jose M. Holgado 19, 2940 Ronda, Malaga
TEL (952) 190 392 **FAX** (952) 190 117
E-MAIL sangabriel@ronda.net **WEBSITE** www.hotelsangabriel.com

We've previously been unexcited by hotels in the much-visited 'white town' of Ronda, so were pleased to get this unequivocal recommendation from a British teacher with a home in southern Spain. He writes:

'In the middle of the old part of town, it's close to the sites that draw the visitors. It was built in 1736, and the handsome old facade has been preserved; inside, there's been a total rebuild to provide 16 individually decorated rooms. On the ground floor are a large drawing room with log-burning stove; a billiards room; and a bar where you have breakfast in the morning and drinks in the evening. It's spotlessly clean, and Jose Manuel Arnal and his familiy are very welcoming, only too pleased to help. A real gem, which captures the style and atmosphere of Ronda brilliantly – you'll feel at home here.'

The Arnal family, who've lived here for many years, opened in 1998 and have evidently succeeded in preserving the authentic feel of an 18thC Spanish house – while providing all the necessary comforts.

∽

Nearby Ronda's bull ring, ravine and historic sites.
Location in side street of old Ronda; free parking in street
Meals breakfast
Price €€€
Rooms 16; 8 double, 8 twin, all with phone, minibar, TV, central heating, air-conditioning
Facilities 3 sitting rooms, library, billiards, video room, concert room, patio, bar
Credit cards AE, MC, V
Children welcome
Disabled suitable
Pets not accepted
Closed never
Proprietors Ilio Perez Giron and José Manuel Arnal

MALAGA

MALAGA

PT DE MALAGA-GIBRALFARO
～ HILLTOP PARADOR ～

Monte de Gibralfaro, 29016, Málaga
TEL 952) 221902 **FAX** (952) 221904
E-MAIL gibralfaro@parador.es **WEBSITE** www.parador.es

If you have time to spare in Málaga, spend it at this Parador, set in the peaceful gardens of the Gibralfaro on a hilltop above the city. It is the setting and the spectacular views, rather than the hotel itself, that make it an exceptional place to stay in this drab concrete port. This Parador is often thronged with people who come up here to escape the heat and hassle, and to enjoy the views of the port and Costa del Sol while they dine on the terraces.

The approach road winds through pine and eucalyptus trees, ending up at an stone-arcaded building, just below the remains of the Phoenician/Moorish castle. Throughly renovated and refurbished in 1995, while tripling the number of its bedrooms, the Parador de Málaga-Gibralfaro has all the usual facilities – spacious bedrooms with large balconies, a busy bar serving excellent snacks, and an attractive dining-room with tables outside under the arches, and the addition of a new outdoor swimming-pool.

Dining up here, with the sea shimmering below you and Gibraltar just visible in the distance, it is hard to believe that you are in the heart of Málaga.

～

Nearby gardens of Gibralfaro, Alcazaba; Costa del Sol.
Location on hill above city, next to castle; with gardens and shaded car parking
Meals breakfast, lunch, dinner
Prices rooms ©©©©; breakfast ©; meals ©©
Rooms 38 double, all with bath; all rooms have central heating, air-conditioning, phone, TV, minibar
Facilities dining-room, sitting-room/bar, terrace, swimming-pool
Credit cards AE, DC, MC, V
Children welcome **Disabled** 1 specially equipped room **Pets** not accepted
Closed never
Manager Juan Carlos García Alonso

MALAGA

BENAOJAN

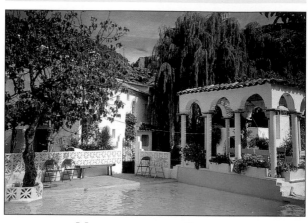

MOLINO DEL SANTO
~ OLD WATER MILL ~

Bda Estación, 29370, Benaoján, Málaga
TEL (952) 167151**FAX** (952) 167327
E-MAIL molino@logiccontrol.es **WEBSITE** www.andalucia.com/molino

A short drive (or train-ride) from Ronda is the sleepy village of Benaoján, perched on a herb-scented mountainside, surrounded by olive and almond groves. Its water-mill, beside the bubbling stream below the village, was converted into a hotel in 1987 by a young English couple, Andy Chapell and Pauline Elkin, who fled the rat-race in favour of this idyllic spot. We could see why as soon as we arrived, on a timeless Sunday morning when the guests were eating a leisurely buffet breakfast under the willow trees on the stone terrace. Dinner is also served out here in the summer (a delicious-sounding set menu with plenty of choice and vegetarian options). To the amusement of the locals, guests also get a real English tea with home-made cakes.

Inside, the rooms are comfortable and home-like; the sitting-area still has some of its original trappings – such as the old grinding stones. The bedrooms vary in size (some take extra beds) and are simply furnished, with bright locally made rugs. Twelve have small terraces overlooking a beautiful swimming-pool, shaded by willow, fig and quince trees.

Andy and Pauline rent out mountain bikes for exploring, and provide information for excursions to all the local sights. We've just heard from a couple who visited three times in three years and still 'can't praise it highly enough.'

~

Nearby cave of La Pileta – paleolithic art; white towns.
Location near railway station; with gardens, car parking
Meals breakfast, lunch, tea, dinner
Prices rooms €€-€€€€€; breakfast €; meals €€ *á la carte*; children's meals
Rooms 17 double all with bath, 5 suites/family rooms; all rooms have central heating, tea and coffee facilities
Facilities dining-room, bar, terrace; solar heated pool
Credit cards AE, DC, MC, V **Children** welcome **Disabled** access difficult **Pets** not accepted **Closed** 19 Nov to 18 Feb **Proprietors** Andy Chapell and Pauline Elkin

MALAGA

OJÉN

REFUGIO DE JUANAR
~ HUNTING LODGE ~

Sierra Blanca, 29610, Ojén, Málaga
TEL (952) 881000 **FAX** (952) 881001

Parador signs still point the way from Ojén to the Refugio in the wild foothills of the Sierra Blanca, although it ceased to be a Parador several years ago. Now run (at least as efficiently as it ever was) by the local authorities, it has become a popular mountain retreat from the pressure of the Costa del Sol – for locals and tourists alike.

It was built as a hunting lodge at the turn of the century and still retains its 'hunting' atmosphere. The sitting-room is an informal jumble of leather sofas around a log fire – deer antlers and zebra skin hang among old English hunting scenes on the walls. Photographs in the bar show wildlife from around the Refugio – ibex and peacocks on the lawns, birds of prey in action. The bedrooms are comfortably rustic and smell of woodsmoke. The restaurant continues on the hunting theme, specializing in game casseroles and local produce. It opens out on to a terrace overlooking pine trees.

Apart from the neat swimming-pool and tennis court, the grounds are wonderfully wild – the perfect place for children of an appropriate age to go exploring. No one with a taste for the outdoors is likely to get bored here.

~

Nearby National Reserve; Ojén (10 km); Marbella (20 km).
Location in mountains, 10 km from Ojen; travelling from Marbella on the main road to Coin, the hotel is signposted at the second exit after Ojen; follow signs to Refugio; with grounds and car parking in drive
Meals breakfast, lunch, dinner
Prices rooms €€-€€€; breakfast €; meals €€
Rooms 18 double, one single, 2 family rooms, 2 suites; all with bath; all rooms have central heating, phone, minibar, TV, safe
Facilities dining-room, sitting-room, TV room, bar; swimming-pool, tennis court, table tennis
Credit cards AE, DC, MC, V **Children** accepted **Disabled** some ground-floor rooms
Pets not accepted **Closed** never **Manager** José Gómez Avila

MALAGA

FINCA LA MOTA
~ COUNTRY INN ~

Partido Urique, 29100, Alhaurín El Grande, Málaga
TEL (952)490901

Behind a high white wall in the lush countryside outside the village of Alhaurín lies this three-hundred-year-old farm-house, now run as a friendly country inn by a British/American combination, Jean and Arun Narang. The hotel's six-acre lawns and shady trees surround a swimming-pool, but for those wanting sand and sea, the Costa del Sol is only a short drive away through the mountains. Most guests prefer the peace of the Andalucian countryside, and enjoy the beautiful walks or rides (on the family ponies) in the surrounding hills.

The rooms at Finca La Mota are pleasantly rustic, with open fires for cold winter days and a mixture of English and Andalucian antiques, collected by the Narangs over the years. Some have four-poster beds. One of our readers who visited recently, however, was disappointed by the quality of the room that he was offered.

The Narangs' restaurant is very popular, offering interesting dishes that are far from the Spanish norm (including Indian and Malaysian curries) and plenty of fresh vegetables from the garden. They are happy to cook guests' special requests and have a big barbecue every weekend.

~

Nearby Coín (10 km); Málaga (25 km).
Location in agricultural countryside about 2 km SW on mijas road out of Alhaurin; with garden and car parking
Meals breakfast, lunch, dinner
Prices rooms €€ with English breakfast; meals €€
Rooms 9 double, 5 with bath; 2 family room with bath; all rooms have tea/coffee kit and electric heaters; all rooms have TV
Facilities dining-room, sitting-room, bar, terrace; swimming-pool, tennis court, mini-golf, riding
Credit cards AE, DC, MC, V
Children welcome **Disabled** 4 ground-floor rooms **Pets** accepted **Closed** never
Proprietors Arun and Jean Narang

MALLORCA

Hotels on the Balearic Islands

The *Islas Baleares* consist of four islands. Largest and most well-known is Mallorca, a popular holiday destination comprising beautiful sandy beaches in the south, and towering mountains, sheer cliffs and rocky coves in the north. One of the island's smartest hotels is on its northern-most point, the Cap de Formentor – the luxurious 127-room Formentor (Tel (971) 899100), splendidly set amidst pine trees on the edge of a beach. It has excellent facilities, especially for children, and comfortable rooms with perfect views of sea and peaks. Deia, close to the rugged north-west coast, has two smart hotels of note; La Residencia (page 182) and the Es Molí, which is stunningly situated on the edge of the cliff. The gardens are luxurious, 'a dazzling array of trailing flowers, laden fruit trees and immaculate lawns, lovingly tended by an army of gardeners'. For those who want to stay nearer Palma, the 60-room Punta Negra (owned by Trusthouse Forte, Tel. (971) 680762) is in a fabulous position on the Costa de Bendinat, away from the hordes but still reasonably convenient. Further away along the south coast, a simple but popular hotel is the Cala Santanyi in the village of the same name. The building is a white arc so that all rooms have a view of one of the most perfect bays imaginable Tel. (971) 165505. Further round the coast is the white holiday complex of Cala d'Or.

Menorca, the smaller neighbour of Mallorca, is a different kettle of fish. Unlike Mallorca, it has escaped mass hotel-building and is still a quiet family holiday island with numerous unspoilt beaches. Of the few hotels, the 82-room Port Mahón is a comfortable, old-fashioned place overlooking the Mahón harbour, praised for its excellent friendly service (Tel (971) 362600); the Rocamar at nearby Cala Fonduco is a restaurant with rooms, providing some of the best seafood on the island and good-value accommodation (Tel (971) 365601).

Ibiza, smaller though more touristy than Menorca, has a Moorish feel to it – the last vestiges of its 8thC occupation. One of the island's few luxury hotels is the Hacienda Na Xamena. The setting is lovely and the facilities are extensive (see page 189). El Palacio (see page 187) is especially for film buffs. Pike's (Tel (971) 342222) is a secluded country house popular with pop stars.

Formentera is a tiny island off the south coast of Ibiza. History and tourism have left it virtually untouched, and it has endless deserted beaches served by a handful of hotels. The choice is mainly between small and simple, such as the 20-room Sa Volta at Es Pujols (Tel (971) 328125), and big and smart, such as the 330-room La Mola at Es Arenals.

MALLORCA

BINISSALEM

SCOTT'S

~ TOWN HOUSE HOTEL ~

Plaza de la Iglesia 12, 07350, Binissalem, Mallorca
TEL (971) 870100 **FAX** (971) 870267
E-MAIL reserve@scottshotel.com **WEBSITE** www.scottshotel.com

Calm, sophistication and unobtrusive luxury are the hallmarks of the new breed of upmarket 'house' hotels which we find in many fashionable cities: now the unspoilt Mallorcan hinterland can boast one as well. Binissalem is the wine capital of the island, a quiet Medieval town ideally situated just 20 minutes from Palma, 30 minutes from beaches and golf clubs on both coasts and close to the island's beautiful mountains.

In keeping with the genre, a discreet brass plaque is the only sign that the elegant former merchant's house in the town's small main square is a hotel. Inside, nothing disappoints; the interior is as calm, sophisticated and unobtrusively luxurious as you could wish, especial attention having been paid to the 16 bedrooms. Each one is different, although they all display the same high standards, with charming fabrics, furniture and pictures, as well as fresh flowers. The beds are top-quality handmade and feel it, with pure cotton sheets and delicious goose-down pillows (synthetic ones are on offer to those who suffer from allergies). A handful of extra bedrooms have been added since our last edition.

Breakfasts are suitably sumptuous, served in the breakfast room or on the terrace.

~

Nearby mountains; Palma 12 miles (19 km).
Location in central square; ample parking
Meals breakfast; light evening meals
Prices rooms ⓔⓔⓔⓔ including breakfast
Rooms 16 double and suites, all with bath; all rooms have central heating, phone, satellite TV/video on request, hairdrier
Facilities 4 sitting rooms, breakfast room, bar/bistro, spa pool, terraces
Credit cards MC, V
Children welcome over 12 **Disabled** access difficult
Pets not accepted **Closed** never
Proprietors George Scott and Judy Brabner Scott

MALLORCA

DEIA

HOTEL LA RESIDENCIA

~ COUNTRY HOTEL ~

Son Canals s/n, 07179, Deia, Mallorca
TEL (971) 639011 **FAX** (971) 639370
E-mail laresidencia@hotel_laresidencia.com **WEBSITE** www.hotel_laresidencia.com

Almost everything about the Residencia (owned by Richard Branson) is out of the ordinary. Set above the road at the north end of the fashionable village of Deia, it is a cluster of creeper-covered stone buildings in beautiful tiered gardens. The core of the hotel is a 16thC manor house; its original olive mill is now the restaurant. There is also an annexe above the swimming-pool behind the main hotel, built in the same pink stone with white shutters.

The interior of the hotel is exquisitely furnished with antique pieces, colourful rugs and fascinating modern art. Bedrooms vary in size – from smallish singles to an enormous suite in a separate building. All have lovely wooden furniture and many have antique or four-poster beds. There are bars and breakfast-rooms in both parts of the hotel, though most people eat out on the terraces overlooking either the swimming-pool (surrounded by elegant cypresses and silver birches) or the front lawns.

Another highlight is the hotel's acclaimed restaurant, El Olivo. Its lofty ceiling, dripping candelabra, cane furniture and elegant tables, set among relics of the olive mill, make a wonderfully romantic setting for an excellent four- or eight-course dinner.

~

Nearby Valldemosa (10 km), Sóller (10 km).
Location Signposted from the road from Deia to Soller ; with garden and car parking
Meals breakfast, lunch, dinner
Prices rooms €€€€ with breakfast; lunch €€, dinner €€€
Rooms 38 double, 8 single, 14 suites (3 with private pool), all with bath; all rooms have central heating, air-conditioning, phone, hairdrier, safe
Facilities 2 restaurants, 4 sitting-rooms, 4 bars, dining-room; 2 outdoor swimming-pools, 1 indoor swimming-pool, 2 tennis courts, private cove; beauty salon, gymnasium, sauna, steam room, spa **Credit cards** AE, MC, V **Children** welcome between 1 to 15 Aug and during Christmas and New Year **Disabled** no special facilities **Pets** small dogs accepted **Closed** never; **Manager** Marie Aastrup

MALLORCA

PORT D'ANDRATX

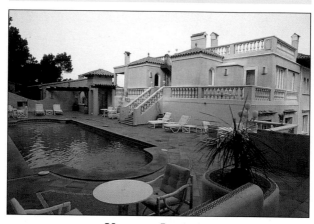

VILLA ITALIA
～ SEASIDE HOTEL ～

Camino de San Carlos, 13, 07157, Port d'Andratx, Mallorca
TEL (971) 674011 **FAX** (971) 673350

From the far side of the bay, the hotel looks very much like a Florentine villa. It was built in the heady 1920s at the whim of an eccentric Italian multimillionaire who wanted to give his lover something more than a string of pearls.

Today Villa Italia is arguably the closest thing to Beverly Hills-on-sea. Politicians, actresses and pop stars have enjoyed a glass of champagne in its swimming-pool and a stroll among the oleanders and palm trees in the gardens.

With its stucco ceilings, Portuguese marble floors, Cretonne curtains, Roman capitals and plinths, mirrors, alabaster chalices, round baths, linen sheets, lace pillows and other hand-made details it is indulgence all the way. For something extra special, if money is no object, book the royal suite.

Service is personal – everything you would expect. An elevator and a small funicular railway transport the luggage to the rooms above.

The area around Andratx (a small, low-key town) is one of the less-developed parts of the Mallorcan coast with some fine cliff-top walks, where Northern Europeans, in particular, will enjoy the specialized and varied wild flowers.

～

Nearby Dragonera Isle (by boat); Palma de Mallorca (22 km).
Location on a slope on the south of the bay, badly signposted; garden and car parking
Meals breakfast, lunch, dinner
Prices rooms €€€€, including breakfast; meals €€
Rooms 10 double, 6 suites, all with bath; all rooms have air-conditioning, telephone, minibar, TV (satellite)
Facilities restaurant; terraces, swimming-pool, sauna
Credit cards AE, MC, V **Children** welcome **Disabled** access difficult
Pets not accepted **Closed** never **Manager** Antonio Martín

MALLORCA

CALA RATJADA

HOTEL SES ROTGES
~ TOWN HOTEL ~

Rafael Blanes 21, 07590, Cala Ratjada, Mallorca
TEL (971) 563108 **FAX** (971) 564345

Some years ago it might have been a surprise to find a well-established French-run hotel in the middle of this village on Mallorca's east coast. Today it would come as no surprise at all – Cala Ratjada is now a lively cosmopolitan holiday town. The Tétards have kept pace with the local development, cleverly extending their pink-stone hotel in the same style as the original buildings, with arched windows and wrought iron balconies.

The hotel, on the corner of two quiet streets near the beach, overlooks a quiet internal courtyard – a wonderful place to relax among trailing plants, overhanging bougainvillaea and a profusion of colourful flowers. The popular restaurant adjoins the courtyard and is set with red and white tables under a beamed roof. In winter, dinner is served inside in another large, cheerful room. The oldest part of the building, around the original chimney, is now a cosy sitting-room. The bedrooms are spacious and airy; they are supposed to be 'individually furnished', but the ones we saw all had the same tiled floors, wooden furniture and bedheads, star-shaped mirrors and modern bathrooms.

Food is a highlight, earning one of the island's very few Michelin stars.

~

Nearby Artà (10 km); Manacor (30 km).
Location in quiet street 200m from beach; with car parking in street
Meals breakfast, lunch, dinner
Prices rooms ©©-©©©©©; breakfast ©©; meals ©©©
Rooms 18 double, 2 single, one family room, 3 suites, all with bath; all rooms have central heating, air-conditioning, phone, TV, safe
Facilities bar, dining-room, sitting-room, TV room, patio
Credit cards AE, DC, MC, V
Children tolerated **Disabled** access generally difficult; one ground-floor room
Pets not accepted **Closed** end Nov to 1 Mar
Proprietor Gérard Charles Tétard

MALLORCA

VALLDEMOSA

VISTAMAR DE VALLDEMOSA

~ COUNTRY HOTEL ~

Carretera Andraitx km2 07170, Valldemosa, Mallorca
TEL (971) 612300 **FAX** (971) 612583
E-MAIL info@vistamarhotel.es **WEBSITE** www.vistamarhotel.es

Vistamar is an appropriate name for this lovely old villa set in country-side on rocky cliffs – you get tantalizing glimpses of the sea through the tangle of pines and olives in front of the hotel. Paths go some way down the cliffs; you cannot get right down to the cove from here, but then you don't really need to – the hotel has its own spectacularly positioned swimming-pool, and is only minutes away from the delightful port of Valldemosa.

A stone archway leads under a balustraded balcony (impressively lit at night) into a cobbled courtyard, with the rooms of the hotel set around three sides. The atmosphere inside is of absolute calm. Rooms are beamed and have heavy wooden doors and antique furniture. Comfortable green and white sofas and chairs are dotted around the two white-walled sitting-rooms, and interesting modern art adds a splash of colour. Dinner is served either inside, or in the partly glassed-in terrace overlooking the gardens.

Bedrooms, some of which have large sun terraces, are cool and comfort-able, with spotless white bathrooms, linen bedcovers and massive wooden cupboards. There are further examples of modern art along the walls of the tall corridors.

Nearby Valldemosa; Bañalbufar (15 km); Deia (15 km)
Location on flat olive plain, 2.5km W of Valldemosa; with garden and car parking
Meals breakfast, lunch, dinner
Prices rooms €€€€ with breakfast; breakfast €; meals €€€
Rooms 19 double, all with bath; all rooms have central heating, phone, TV, minibar; a few rooms have jacuzzi
Facilities dining-rooms, sitting-rooms, bar, terrace; swimming-pool
Credit cards AE, DC, MC, V
Children accepted **Disabled** access difficult **Pets** not accepted
Closed Nov to Jan **Proprietor** Pedro Coll

MALLORCA

ORIENT

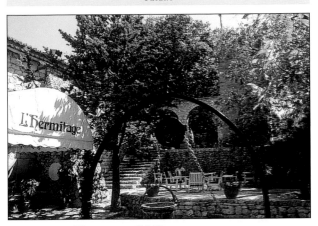

HOTEL L'HERMITAGE
~ COUNTRY HOTEL ~

07349, Orient, Mallorca
TEL (971) 180303 **FAX** (971) 180411

THE GREAT ATTRACTION of L'Hermitage is its setting – tucked away in a beautiful fruit-growing valley in the mountains, miles from the beaten track (no mean achievement in Mallorca). It consists of a somewhat strange selection of buildings: a narrow 17thC stone manor house (with tower), a two-storey modern block overlooking an orchard and a totally separate cloister with 16 twisted stone pillars enclosing lemon and orange trees. Only four of the bedrooms are in the old house. These have tiny windows peering out of thick walls, making the rooms beautifully cool but also very dim; with polished furniture on old tiled floors, they have much more character than the modern rooms – though these are also cool and comfortable, with palatial bathrooms.

There is a warren of tiny public rooms in the old part of the hotel, including an elegant downstairs sitting-room and a cosy upstairs one with an open fire. In contrast, the dining-room in the old olive mill is enormous. It still has a sloping, beamed ceiling and the original grinding-stones, which make an admirable table for the generous buffet breakfasts.

There is a heated terrace on which meals can be enjoyed outside even if the weather is cool. Freshly baked cakes and tarts are available at tea-time.

~

NEARBY Buñola (10 km), Alaró (10 km).
LOCATION in fruit-orchard valley in mountains, 1km E of Orient; with garden and car parking
MEALS buffet breakfast, snacks, lunch, tea, dinner
PRICES rooms €€€€; breakfast €; meals *á la carte*
ROOMS 24 double, all with bath; all rooms have central heating, phone, minibar; some rooms have TV, safe, hairdrier**FACILITIES** dining-room, 2 sitting-rooms, bar, terrace; sauna, 2 tennis court, heated swimming-pool **CREDIT CARDS** AE, DC, MC, V
CHILDREN accepted **DISABLED** no special facilities **PETS** not accepted
CLOSED Nov to Feb **MANAGER** Erna Tietz

IBIZA

IBIZA

El Palacio

~ Town hotel ~

Calle de la Conquista, 2, Ibiza, Baleares
Tel (971) 301478 **Fax** (971) 391581

The Hotel of the Movie Stars', El Palacio is a Mecca for film buffs. Every room is named after a legendary Hollywood star. A recent reporter noted superb bedroom views, white leather sofas and antique furniture. It is a converted mansion in the city's old quarter (peaceful, but five minutes' walk from the nightlife), decorated throughout with posters, photographs and movie memorabilia, including the only award James Dean received in his lifetime. The hotel's brochure describes not only every room, but also gives the biographies of the eponymous stars and the history of the objects on display. A small pond and a trickling fountain create a tranquil atmosphere in the courtyard garden.

~

Nearby Dalt Vila (old town), Playas Salinas (5 km).
Location in a quiet street in the old town; car parking on street
Meals breakfast, snacks
Prices rooms €€€€ including breakfast
Rooms 7 suites, all with bath; all rooms have balcony or terrace. 'Marilyn' is a penthouse suite
Facilities sitting-rooms/foyer with video, bar; garden
Credit cards AE, DC, V **Children** accepted **Disabled** access difficult
Pets small ones only **Closed** Nov to Mar **Proprietor** Marlise Etienne

---

READERS' REPORTS

Please write and tell us about your experiences of small hotels, guest-houses and inns, whether good or bad, whether listed in this edition or not. As well as hotels in Spain, we are interested in hotels in Britain and Ireland, Italy, France, Portugal, Austria, Switzerland, Germany and other European countries, and those in the eastern United States.

The address to write to is:

The Editor,
Charming Small Hotel Guides
c/o Duncan Petersen Publishing Ltd,
31 Ceylon Road,
London W14 OPY.

To the hundreds of readers who have written with comments on hotels in all the *Charming Small Hotel Guides*, a sincere 'thank-you'. We attach great importance to your comments and absorb them into the text each year. Please keep writing: for further information see page 12.

IBIZA

LES TERRASSES

~ COUNTRY HOTEL ~

Apartado 1235, Carretera de S. Eulàlia – km 1, 07800 Santa Eulàlia del Río, Ibiza
TEL (971) 332643 **FAX** (971) 338978
E-MAIL lesterrasses@interbook.es **WEBSITE** lesterrasses.net

A vivid cobalt blue rock 1 km south of Santa Eulàlia, marks the country track which leads up to this enchanting *finca*. Without losing the simplicity of its farmhouse origins, Françoise Pialoux, who is French, has embellished Les Terrasses with great panache. Everyday items, such as a jar of preserved fruit, a plant pot or an ironwork chair are perfectly placed, wall colours are exquisite. As the name suggests, the main house, bedrooms (in a separate building) and gardens are on different terraced levels. So are the two secluded swimming-pools. Crisp, white bedlinen in the plainly furnished bedrooms is offset by walls painted in hues of ochre, blue or pink; recessed baths and tiled shower areas, which form an integral part of the rooms, suggest an exotic, North African influence. Meals are taken outside on the main terrace, or in the yellow dining-room. On some evenings couscous dishes are served.

Hammocks, padded benches, sofas, tables and chairs adorn the many unexpected little patios, shady nooks and peaceful courtyards. They make enticing spots in which to while away a lazy afternoon; more than anything they endorse the private villa atmosphere.

~

Nearby Santa Eulàlia del Río (3 km), Ibitha Town (Eivissa) (9 km).
Location between Ibitha Town (Eivissa) and Santa Eulàlia; large gardens, ample car parking
Meals breakfast, lunch, dinner
Prices €€€€
Rooms 9 double, all with bath, phone, minibar, air-conditioning
Facilities sitting-room, dining-room, breakfast-room, garden; two swimming pools, tennis
Credit cards V
Children welcome **Disabled** not suitable **Pets** accepted
Closed 15 Nov to 20 Dec
Proprietor Françoise Pialoux

IBIZA

SAN MIGUEL

HOTEL HACIENDA NA XAMENA

~ CLIFFTOP HOTEL ~

Na Xamena, San Miguel, Ibiza 07800
TEL (971) 334500 FAX (971) 334514
E-MAIL hotelhacienda@retemail.es

Reached by one of the prettiest lanes on Ibiza, Hotel Hacienda also enjoys one of the most fortunate locations on the island, and is surrounded by crags and pine woods. The terrace around a large, curvacious swimming-pool hangs over a spectacular, rocky cove which is accessible only by a scramble. (There are two others – one, indoor and heated.) The hotel is built in bright, white Ibizenco style, complemented by natural materials such as rocks and shady palm fronds, with many arches and rounded corners, and is arranged around a central patio. Solid chunks of wood and massive wooden beams create an impressive effect in the bar area. Bedrooms are downstairs, and each has a terrace or balcony (except for single rooms) and magnificent views. Some have whirlpool baths situated beside enormous windows which directly overlook the sea. The poolside restaurant, Las Cascadas, is ideal for watching the sun go down while dining, and has an enviable local reputation. El Sueno de Estrellas, the other restaurant, is more intimate, and decorated in Arab style.

A luxurious and secluded place in which to take refuge from the tourist traps of Ibiza. The native flora and fauna can be discovered through guided hiking tours into the surrounding hills.

~

Nearby Can Marça cave; Ibiza (23 km).
Location a left turning before the port of San Miguel; car parking
Meals breakfast, lunch, dinner
Prices rooms €€€€; breakfast €€; meals €€€
Rooms 37 double, 5 single, 10 suites; all rooms have central heating, air-conditioning, telephone, minibar, radio, TV (satellite)
Facilities 2 restaurants, bar; discotheque; 3 swimming-pools (one heated), steam room, sauna, tennis-court, mountain bikes
Credit cards AE, DC, MC, V
Children welcome **Disabled** access possible **Pets** accepted in room only
Closed Nov to Easter Week **Manager** Sabine Lipszyc

LANZAROTE

CASERIO DE MOZAGA

~ VILLAGE HOTEL ~

Mozaga, 8, 35562 San Bartolomé, Lanzarote
TEL (928) 520060 **FAX** (928) 522029

Gonzalo Bèthencourt's 200-year-old *finca* is just the place to savour some of the oddities that make Lanzarote an island like no other. The farmhouse – painted the island's regulation white and green – sits in a scruffy, windswept, inland village, a world away from the seaside resorts. In an adjacent field, Gonzalo grows palms and drago plants in soil covered in picûn, a grey volcanic gravel used by locals to keep the earth underneath moist. More ancient methods of dealing with the island's scarcity of water are evident in a rock terrace incised with rivulets to catch the infrequent rain, and a traditional water purifier in the form of a chunk of lava rock set over an old urn.

Most bedrooms are set around a pretty geranium-decorated courtyard centred on an old well. Rugs on wooden floors, shutters and country antiques such as a chunky washstand or potty cabinet imbue them with lots of character. This is very much a place where you feel part of a home. Breakfasts (generous buffets) and dinners (set meals featuring local vegetables and fresh fish) are eaten at one large table, together with other guests and maybe Gonzalo – who speaks good English - and his sister Maria Luisa.

~

Nearby La Casa Museo del Campesino (1 km); Teguise (8 km); Fundaciûn Cèsar Manrique (11 km).
Location on the edge of the village; ample parking
Meals breakfast, dinner
Prices rooms €€€-€€€€, including breakfast; dinner €€
Rooms 5 double, 1 single, 2 suites, all with bath; all rooms have TV, phone, minibar
Facilities sitting-room, dining-room **Credit cards** AE, DC, M, V
Children welcome **Disabled** most rooms on ground floor
Pets not accepted **Closed** never
Owner Gonzalo Rodrigues Bèthencourt

LANZAROTE

YAIZA

FINCA DE LAS SALINAS
VILLAGE HOTEL

Calle La Cuesta, 17, 35570, Yaiza, Lanzarote
TEL (928) 830325 **FAX** (928) 830329

Cèsar Manrique, the artist/architect who ensured that Lanzarote should be largely spared from ugly tourist development, would surely have approved of the bold, classy conversion of this 18thC finca. Public areas are ranged around the little mansion – a Moorish folly of a building, with low, castellated turrets. Its two patios – one still open to the elements with palms sprouting skywards – have been turned into stylish sitting areas, decked out with modern art and white-cushioned wicker armchairs. Appropriately, the room where grapes were once crushed (the old machinery has been retained) now serves as the bar. Most bedrooms lie in the former stable block. They are modern rustic in design, with washed blue, yellow or lime green walls, wrought-iron beds, wacky bedside lamps and stainless steel bathroom sinks set into glass tops. Each has a private terrace, enclosed by lava walls, and overlooks a slick swimming-pool surrounded by a boarded deck.

The pretty village of Yaiza stands right on the edge of Lanzarote's malpals or volcanic badlands. The island's most charming restaurant, La Era, converted (by Manrique) from another old farmhouse, is a short walk down the road from the hotel.

Nearby Parque Nacional de Timanfaya (19 km); resorts of Puerto del Carmen and Playa Blanca (15 km).
Location on the edge of the village; ample parking
Meals breakfast, dinner
Prices rooms €€€-€€€€€, including breakfast; dinner €€
Rooms 17 double, 2 suites, all with bath; all rooms have central heating, TV (satellite), radio, phone, air-conditioning, minibar
Facilities bar, sitting-room, dining-room, swimming-pool, games room, tennis, gym, sauna **Credit cards** AE, DC, M, V **Children** accepted, but no child discounts
Disabled all bedrooms on ground floor, but none adapted **Pets** not accepted
Closed never **Owner** Maria Carmen Lleo

TENERIFE

GARACHICO

SAN ROQUE
~ SEASIDE VILLAGE HOTEL ~

Calle Esteban de Ponte, 32, 38450, Garachico, Tenerife
TEL (922) 133435 **FAX** (922) 133406

Hands-on owners Dominique Carayon, a Frenchman, and his Spanish wife Laly have created nothing less than a tour de force of modernist elegance, wrapped up in a grand 17thC mansion. Set around two wooden-galleried patios (one containing the swimming-pool), the building itself is a treat, with walls painted a rich russet, and floors of honey-coloured Canarian pine. But the eye is drawn to the startling modern art – say the giant steel sculpture of a grasshopper in the main patio – and the many pieces of original Bauhaus furniture, copied under licence. With their pitched roofs, more beautiful wood floors, interesting art and furniture, bedrooms are as stylish as the rest of the enterprise. They also come with indulgent mod-cons, such as CD and video players. Don't be put off if it all sounds intimidatingly swanky: the Carayons ensure that the atmosphere is thoroughly easy-going.

In the evening, modern jazz wafts through the candlelit patios, and Laly's set dinners are served at the poolside (if breakfasts are anything to go by, they should be top-notch). But there is no pressure to eat in. Little Garachico – a beguiling, ancient seaside backwater that was once Tenerife's most important port – has half-a-dozen fish restaurants to choose from.

~

Nearby Puerto de la Cruz (26km); Parque Nacional del Tiede (57km).
Location on quiet back street near the village centre; easy street parking
Meals breakfast, lunch, dinner
Prices rooms ⓔⓔⓔⓔ, including breakfast; meals ⓔⓔ
Rooms 16 double, 4 suites, all with bath; all have central heating, TV (satellite), phone, air-conditioning, minibar, Jacuzzis
Facilities sitting-room, swimming-pool, sauna, fishing rods and mountain bikes for hire
Credit cards AE, DC, M, V **Children** welcome **Disabled** no special facilities
Pets accepted **Closed** never **Owners** Laly and Dominique Carayon

TENERIFE

PARQUE NACIONAL DEL TIEDE

PT CAÑADAS DEL TIEDE
~ MODERN PARADOR ~

Las Cañadas del Tiede, 38300 La Orotava, Tenerife
TEL (922) 386415 **FAX** (922) 382352

This parador has arguably the most extraordinary location of any hotel in Spain. The only proper building for miles around, it stands within an enormous volcanic crater – a bizarre jumble of chocolate-brown and red rubble and weirdly-shaped rocks – and towering over it is the cone of Mount Tiede, Spain's highest peak. The hotel is most enjoyable when the day-trippers who descend on its cafeteria and park information centre have departed. Come evening, the setting sun turns the landscape a deep orange, and at night the clear air reveals a firmament of a thousand stars.

Styled as a plush mountain chalet, the parador has recently undergone a much-needed revamp. Bedrooms (try to bag one with a view of Mount Tiede) are very comfortable and understated, with Canarian pine floors, dark wood furniture, and swish marble bathrooms. Spacious, open-plan public areas capitalise on the views, and feature a large selection of prints showing Tenerife's stunning scenery. Expect good food, in the form of mammoth buffet breakfasts, and hearty dinners that concentrate on Canarian specialities such as rabbit and goat stews. To work up an appetite, you can follow two circular walks through the crater that start from the hotel's front door. ~

Nearby cable car up Mount Tiede (3 km); La Orotava (42 km).
Location in heart of national park; with car park
Meals breakfast, lunch, dinner
Prices rooms €€€€€; breakfast €, meals €€-€€€
Rooms 34 double, 1 single, 2 suites, all with bath; all rooms have central heating, TV (satellite), phone, minibar
Facilities bar, sitting-room, dining-room, cafeteria, indoor swimming-pool, gym, sauna **Credit cards** AE, DC, M, V **Children** welcome
Disabled lift/elevator; 1 bedroom adapted **Pets** not accepted
Closed never
Manager Jesus Garrido Pozo

HOTEL NAMES

Hotels are arranged in order of the most distinctive part of their name; other parts of the name are also given, except that very common prefixes such as 'Hotel' and 'La' are omitted. The abbreviation PT is used for Parador de Turismo de España (see Introduction for further explanation). Hotels covered in the several Area introductions, and in the feature boxes on Paradores, are not indexed.

HOTEL NAMES

HOTEL NAMES

Hotel Names

HOTEL NAMES

HOTEL LOCATIONS

In this index, hotels are arranged by the name of the city, town or village they are in or near. Where a hotel is located in a very small place, it may be indexed under a nearby place which is more easily found on maps. The abbreviation PT is used for Parador de Turismo de España (see Introduction for further explanation).

HOTEL LOCATIONS

HOTEL LOCATIONS

Hotel Locations

Hotel Locations

HOTEL LOCATIONS

SPECIAL OFFERS

Buy your *Charming Small Hotel Guide* by post directly
from the publisher and you'll get a worthwhile discount. *

Titles available:	Retail price	Discount price
Austria	£10.99	£9.50
Britain	£11.99	£10.50
France	£11.99	£10.50
France: Bed & Breakfast	£10.99	£9.50
Germany	£9.99	£8.50
Greece	£10.99	£9.50
Ireland	£9.99	£8.50
Italy	£11.99	£10.50
Paris	£10.99	£9.50
Southern France	£10.99	£9.50
Switzerland	£9.99	£8.50
Tuscany & Umbria	£10.99	£9.50
USA: New England	£10.99	£9.50
Venice and North-East Italy	£10.99	£9.50

Please send your order to:

Book Sales,

Duncan Petersen Publishing Ltd,

31 Ceylon Road, London W14 OPY

enclosing: 1) the title you require and number of copies

2) your name and address

3) your cheque made out to:

Duncan Petersen Publishing Ltd

*Offer applies to this edition and to UK only.

Visit charmingsmallhotels.co.uk
Our website has expanded enormously since its launch and continues to grow. It's the best research tool on the web for our kind of hotel.

Exchange rates
As we went to press, $1 bought 1.02 euros and £1 bought 1.58 euros